frame*work*

TEN ARCHITECTURAL KNITS

Norah Gaughan

QUINCE & CO

PORTLAND, MAINE

Published in 2017 by
Quince & Company
142 High Street
Suite 220
Portland, ME 04101

ISBN 978-0-9861039-9-5

Printed in the US by a wind-powered printer
on US-made paper

FSC
www.fsc.org
MIX
Paper from
responsible sources
FSC® C102465

PRINTED WITH
100% WIND ENERGY

table of
CONTENTS

Foreword

This is a book of sweater designs. It's also a book about sweater design, in particular how one designer uses simple geometric shapes to structure and embellish her knitwear.

I have long been an admirer of Norah Gaughan. Before the phrase *outside the box* came into common usage, Norah was imagining sweaters and stitches in ways very much her own. For example, her book *Knitting Nature* (Stewart, Tabori & Chang, 2006) is a collection of pieces whose stitches and structure are based on hexagons, spirals, and pentagons, forms found over and over in nature.

In this collection, Norah looks at how simple geometric shapes—rectangles, triangles, and circles—can provide a framework for thinking about sweater design in both stitch invention and sweater structure. Take, for example, Gambrel (page 70). In this piece, Norah took a simple fitted top (a rectangle with waist shaping) and cut out large circles for armholes. She picked up stitches around this circle edge for sleeves and, by working straight rows of alternating stitch patterns in two different yarns, she emphasized the concentric circle structure of the armholes/sleeves.

As geometric pieces can fit together in puzzle fashion, in the flowing Arena (page 34), Norah built her cardigan in pieces, all of them picked up from an existing edge, with few seams. Beginning with a small vertical panel at the back neck, she worked the yoke outward to cover front and back, then knitted fronts, back, and sleeves out or down from the yoke.

The pieces in *Framework* can also be seen as a way to explore the rectangle in sweater silhouette. Our torsos are tubes, more or less. Anything that covers us is, essentially, a tube when worn and a rectangle when laying flat. Imagining how a basic rectangle can morph to follow the lines of our bodies is another theme in this book, one that she explores on pages 78 and 79.

Though some of these sweaters may look tricky, once you understand how the pieces fit together, the moves you need to make them become simple and obvious. We hope that by knitting one or more of these pieces, or simply by studying how they're made, you'll soon be thinking about how to take a simple knitted rectangle and tweak it to make something new and different.

Pam Allen

Introduction

Linen is one of my favorite fibers, but I know it sometimes gets overlooked in the knitting world. A bit of patience and faith in your fiber pays off after your stitches hit the water. If you've never worked with linen before—even if you have—you'll find useful pointers on knitting with this timeless and lovely fiber on pages 8 and 9.

Over the last few years I've been playing around with geometric shapes as simple as rectangles, triangles, and circles while pushing the concept of fit. I used to think of most sweaters in terms of pieces—front(s), back, and sleeves. I've since come to realize how wonderfully one large shape can envelope the body. A rectangle with two slits can be a lovely draped vest. A circle with sleeves becomes a rounded-hem jacket with a shawl collar. The idea of fit becomes very fluid with these pieces. Although the patterns are written in several sizes, each will fit a wide variety of women. You may find yourself picking a size based more on your preferred length rather than its, or your, width. In *Framework*, several pieces are each made from a single geometric shape. The Dormer poncho and Cella shrug show this idea in its simplest form. Each is made from a single rectangle.

The next step in my design evolution with geometric shapes was to carve away or bump out a few details, like necklines and armholes, with increases and decreases. For instance, Walkway's front piece starts out as a large rectangle. Then, decreases create the deep V-neck while increases form a bit of a cap sleeve. It's as if the rectangle was slit in the center and each side bent outward. Bower is a similarly simple deviation away from a starting big rectangle. One slender triangle is removed to form the center front opening and back neck. On top of the basic structure, a few extra details, such as the leaf motifs, are added.

Interesting garments can also be created by adding geometric shapes onto each other or onto more typical sweater pieces. One example is Annex. A typical sleeveless tank in its basic shape, the bottom corners are carved out making way for rectangle pieces placed in their stead, forming peplum-like extensions. In a slightly different approach, Arris is built of rectangles and triangles, angled to form the fitted, more typical, silhouette.

I love how modern these pieces feel to me, too, even though these shapes have been used in traditional clothing for centuries. One more thing: In this collection, in addition to exploring shapes, I reduced the number of seams making things as seamless as possible while keeping them easy to knit. I hope you find them equally enjoyable to knit and to wear.

Norah

Linen

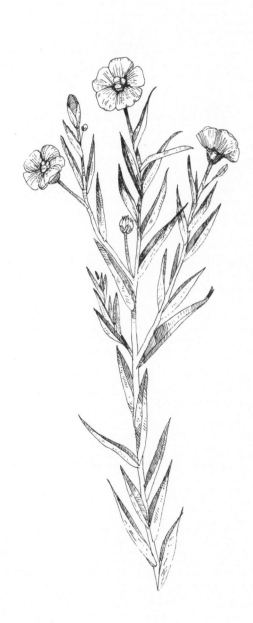

The linen fiber used to spin yarn comes from flax, a tall, slender plant that blooms in spring with a pretty blue flower. The fibers, taken from an inner part of the stem, are long, relative to wool fibers, a property that makes linen extremely durable and strong. A linen garment only improves with wear. It can take lots of machine washing and drying with ease and becomes more soft and lovely with time.

Linen's long staple gives yarn a soft sheen; the long unbroken surface reflects more light than wool or cotton's short fibers. And given that linen is stable and inelastic—the strand has no give—a linen garment's shape stays put; it won't stretch out and down as you wear it. Another benefit: Linen is quite literally cool to wear. Its hollow fibers absorb moisture which then evaporates, cooling things around it, namely you.

These are all reasons to love knitting with linen. That said, here are a few things to be aware of before you cast on.

Knit a large swatch and avoid surprises. You already know the importance of a gauge swatch. (Right?) But when you're working with linen yarn, it's really, really important to take your swatch seriously because gauge in linen can change significantly when it's blocked. It might not, but there's only one way to know.

A large six- or eight-inch square will tell you a lot about how your finished piece will behave, so take the time to knit one up. After knitting the swatch (in the designated stitch pattern) and before blocking it, lay it out and carefully measure it, noting the numbers. Then block your swatch in exactly the same way you plan to handle your sweater. Whether you hand wash and wet block your swatch, or use the gentle cycle on your washing machine and toss it in the dryer, be sure your swatch is completely dry before measuring. You might even tape it to the wall overnight to see if it will behave differently when worn. Make notes of any changes you notice and use the blocked-swatch numbers as your gauge.

Linen doesn't behave like wool when you're knitting. Linen is less forgiving than wool. Its inelasticity means linen remembers everything. Stitches are more slippery, and might appear uneven. Your hands may get tired if you try to snug up your stitches. If so, loosen up and try to let go of that need for perfection. Things will even out when you block. If your stitches still seem sloppy, don't fret. Keep your hands relaxed and go down a needle size or two to tighten things up. Your hands will thank you.

Weave in your ends with care. Since linen makes a smooth yarn, it doesn't have the barbs and crimps that allow wool ends to grab onto stitches and mesh with them, to prevent unraveling. Linen ends need to be woven for longer distances in this plant fiber, especially if using a machine to wash or dry. Use duplicate stitch (page 81) so the tail will mimic the knitted stitches and not affect the flexibility or drape of the fabric, and cut the tail ends longer than you would for wool to keep them from slipping back along the woven path.

Linen can sometimes bias. Depending on how you knit, a linen piece in stockinette stitch may lean slightly to the left or right. This is a tendency exaggerated when knitting in the round. Garments knitted in separate pieces, or which have a loose and swingy shape will live happily with a little tilt of the stitches.

For more information on knitting with linen, the websites below are a good place to start:
marvelknits.wordpress.com/2015/06/11/knitting-with-linen-technicalities
quinceandco.com/blogs/news/114693766-warming-up-to-linen
untangling-knots.com/2016/05/20/6-things-to-know-about-knitting-with-linen
knitbot.com/blog/2013/5/22/finishing-with-linen

And for a list of other helpful links and tutorials, visit our blog at quinceandco.com.

framework

TEN KNITWEAR DESIGNS

Perimeter

Last seen in the 1970s, summer scarves posing as necklaces have resurfaced as a trend. My version, Perimeter, is simply a long rectangle made open and light with eyelets. Long twisted fringe helps weigh down the lace a bit. The two sides are barely distinguishable—there's no real right or wrong side—so it's no matter when your lariat blows in the breeze.

FINISHED MEASUREMENTS
2" [5 cm] wide and 45" [114.5] long, before fringe

YARN
Sparrow by Quince & Co
(100% organic linen; 168yd [155m]/50g)
1 skein Paprika 210

NEEDLES
One pair in size US 4 [3.5 mm]
Or size to obtain gauge

NOTIONS
Crochet hook in size B [2.25 mm]
or C [2.75 mm]
Tapestry needle

GAUGE
14 sts and 12 rows = 2" [5 cm]
in stitch pattern, after wet blocking.

CONSTRUCTION NOTES
This little lariat scarf uses four kinds of yarnovers: Between a purl and a knit stitch, a knit and a purl stitch, two purl stitches and two knit stitches (page 15). The size of your yarnover may vary, depending on which kinds of stitches, knit or purl, fall on either side of it. You probably don't need to worry about slight differences in eyelet size, but if you're a yarnover perfectionist, find a tip on page 15 to help you to make consistent eyelets.

STITCH PATTERN
Eyelet pattern (14 stitches)
Row 1: (WS) K1, p2, k2tog, yo, p2, yo, p2tog, yo, ssk, p2, k1.
Row 2: K1, yo, ssk, p2, k2, yo, ssk, p2, k2tog, yo, k1.
Repeat Rows 1 and 2 for eyelet pattern.
(For details on how to make yarnovers, see page 15.)

LARIAT
Using the long-tail cast on, CO 14 sts.

Begin stitch pattern
First row: (WS) Work Row 1 of eyelet pattern to end.
Cont in patt until pc meas 45" [114 cm] from beg.
Next row: Bind off knitwise.

FINISHING
Weave in ends. Wet block lariat to finished measurements.
Add twisted fringe (page 14).

TWISTED FRINGE

Cut 30 strands of yarn in 19" [48.5 cm] lengths.

TIP: Wrap yarn around a 9" [23 cm] tall hardcover book or piece of sturdy cardboard cut to the right size 30 times, then cut through all strands at one end.

Place five twisted fringe at each narrow end of the scarf, one on each corner, one in the middle, and two evenly spaced between corners and center.

HOW TO MAKE TWISTED FRINGE

For each fringe, hold three strands together, aligning ends. (Fig 1) At narrow end of scarf, insert hook into designated space from back to front. Fold yarn in half over the hook, and draw down through the hole for approx 2" [5 cm]. (Fig 2, left to right.) Open up the space between the folded strands, and draw all six yarn ends through together. Draw the knot up until it's snug against the fabric's edge. Repeat as specified at each fringe position.

Secure one fringe knot to a blocking board or upholstered surface with one or two straight pins. Divide the six strands into two sets of three. Tape one set down (or secure in your hand, if you like). Twist the other set counter-clockwise by rolling between your fingers. Once it's fully twisted, tape it down or secure in your hand, careful not to lose the twist. Repeat for second set of strands. Holding one twisted strand in each hand, twist together clockwise by passing them between your hands, left strand over right, until strands are fully twisted (approx 30 passes). Knot approx 1" [2.5 cm] from end and trim.

Repeat for each piece of fringe.

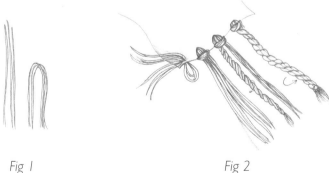

Fig 1   *Fig 2*

HOW TO MAKE YARNOVERS

Fig 1

Knit to purl stitch: Bring yarn between needles to the front, then over the RH needle and between needles to the front again before purling the next stitch. (Fig 1)

Purl to purl stitch: Bring yarn over RH needle to the back and then between needles to the front again before purling the next stitch. (Fig 2)

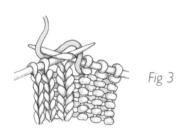

Fig 2

Purl to knit stitch: With yarn in front, knit next stitch; yarn passes over needle to create yarnover. (Fig 3)

Knit to knit stitch: Bring yarn between needles to the front, then knit the next stitch, yarn crosses over RH needle to create yarnover. (Fig 4)

TIP for yarnover perfectionists:
Yarnover openings can vary in size depending on how you knit and which kind of stitches, knit or purl, fall on each side. The shorter the distance the yarn travels between bordering stitches, the smaller the eyelet opening. To make yarnovers larger, try wrapping the yarn clockwise (looking down on the point) around the needle, instead of counter-clockwise:

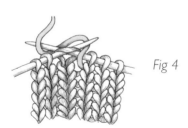

Fig 3

For example, to make a **purl to knit** yarnover larger, bring the yarn between the needles to the back, then over the needle and between them to the back again, ready to knit the next stitch. (Fig 5)

To make a **knit to knit** yarnover larger, bring the yarn over the RH needle, then between needles to the back, ready to knit the next stitch.

When you wrap a yarnover clockwise around the needle, you'll need to knit or purl into the back of the yarnover on the next row. Wrapping clockwise creates a stitch that faces in a direction opposite the usual. If you work it through the front of the loop, as you do your other stitches, you'll create a twisted stitch.

Note: Illustrations show technique worked in stockinette stitch. For Perimeter, work the yarnovers in designated stitch pattern.

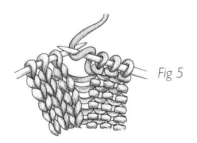

Fig 5

Dormer

Even as the designer I have a hard time deciding if Dormer is a pullover or a poncho. The basic rectangle construction allows you to concentrate on the pattern stitch, a combination of a cable within a cable and columns of dropped stitches, which form long ladders. The piece could easily be made into a pullover. Simply sew up the sides. Work more rows on the cuffs for longer, fitted sleeves.

FINISHED MEASUREMENTS
39¼ (45¾)" [99.5 (116) cm] wide
and 30 (36)" [76 (91.5) cm] long,
shown in size 39¼" [99.5 cm]
on 34" [86.5 cm] model

YARN
Kestrel by Quince & Co
(100% organic linen; 76yd [70 m]/50g)
9 (13) skeins Anemone 513

NEEDLES
One 32" circular needle in
size US 9 [5.5 mm]
One set double-pointed needles in
size US 7 [4.5 mm]
Or size to obtain gauge

NOTIONS
Stitch marker
Cable needle
Locking stitch markers
Tapestry needle

GAUGE
16 sts and 24 rows = 4" [10 cm]
in stockinette stitch, after wet blocking
One cable pattern repeat =
3¼" [8.5 cm] wide and 2¼" [5.5 cm] tall,
after blocking.

CONSTRUCTION NOTES
Dormer is knitted in one piece from side to side. To make the neckline slit, front and back are separated at the shoulder and worked separately to the opposite shoulder, then joined and worked as one piece to the opposite cuff edge. When knitting is complete, designated stitches are dropped to the bottom edge of the piece to form ladders. Then cuffs are picked up and knitted.

SPECIAL ABBREVIATIONS
C6B (cable 6 back, leans to the right): Slip 3 stitches onto cable needle (cn) and hold in back, k3, then k3 from cn.
C6F (cable 6 front, leans to the left): Slip 3 stitches onto cn and hold in front, k3, then k3 from cn.
C8B (cable 8 back, leans to the right): Slip 4 stitches onto cn and hold in back, k4, then k4 from cn.
C8F (cable 8 front, leans to the left): Slip 4 stitches onto cn and hold in front, k4, then k4 from cn.
yo2 (yarn over twice / double yarnover): Bring yarn over needle twice.

DORMER RIGHT CABLE

12
11
10
9
8
7
6
5
4
3
2
1

13-stitch repeat

DORMER LEFT CABLE

12
11
10
9
8
7
6
5
4
3
2
1

13-stitch repeat

KEY

☐	knit on RS, purl on WS
●	purl on RS, knit on WS
○	yo
╱	k2tog
╲	ssk
	C6B
	C6F
	C8B
	C8F
☐	pattern repeat

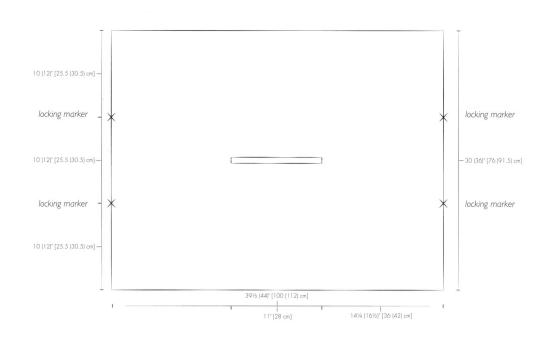

10 (12)" [25.5 (30.5) cm]

locking marker

10 (12)" [25.5 (30.5) cm]

locking marker

10 (12)" [25.5 (30.5) cm]

30 (36)" [76 (91.5) cm]

locking marker

locking marker

39½ (44)" [100 (112) cm]

11" [28 cm]   14¼ (16½)" [36 (42) cm]

STITCH PATTERNS

Right cable pattern (multiple of 13 stitches + 5)

Row 1: (RS) K2, p1, yo, ssk, *p1, k2tog, yo, k2, C6B, yo, ssk; rep from * to marker (m)/last st.

Row 2 and all WS rows: *P12, k1; rep from * to last 5 sts, p2, k3.

Row 3: K2, p1, yo, ssk, *p1, k2tog, yo, k8, yo, ssk; rep from * to m/last st.

Rows 5 and 7: Rep Row 3.

Row 9: K2, p1, yo, ssk, *p1, k2tog, yo, C8B, yo, ssk; rep from * to m/last st.

Row 11: Rep Row 3.

Row 12: (WS) Rep Row 2.

Repeat Rows 1-12 for right cable pattern.

Left cable pattern (multiple of 13 stitches + 5)

Row 1: (RS) *K2tog, yo, C6F, k2, yo, ssk, p1; rep from * to last 5 sts, k2tog, yo, p1, k2.

Row 2 and all WS rows: K3, p2, *k1, p12; rep from * to 1 st before m/last st.

Row 3: *K2tog, yo, k8, yo, ssk, p1; rep from * to last 5 sts, k2tog, yo, p1, k2.

Rows 5 and 7: Rep Row 3.

Row 9: *K2tog, yo, C8F, yo, ssk, p1; rep from * to last 5 sts, k2tog, yo, p1, k2.

Row 11: Rep Row 3.

Row 12: (WS) Rep Row 2.

Repeat Rows 1-12 for left cable pattern.

PONCHO

Beg at cuff edge, with larger needle, and using the long-tail cast on, CO 133 (163) sts. Do not join.

Begin pattern set up

Set up row 1: (WS) K3, p2, *BO 3 sts (1 st rem on RH needle tip), p11; rep from * 7 (9) more times, BO 3 sts (1 st rem on RH needle tip), p1, k3; 27 (33) sts dec'd—106 (130) sts rem.

Set up row 2: K2, p1, yo, ssk, *yo2, k2tog, yo, k8, yo, ssk; rep from * 7 (9) more times, yo2, k2tog, yo, p1, k2.

Set up row 3: K3, p2, (k1 into yo2, dropping second yo, p12) 4 (5) times, k1 into yo2, dropping second yo, place marker (pm), (p12, k1 into yo2, dropping second yo) 4 (5) times, p2, k3—115 (141) sts.

Begin stitch pattern

Next row: (RS) Work Row 1 of right cable pattern to marker (m), slip marker (sl m), p1, work Row 1 of left cable pattern to end.

Next row: Work next row of left cable patt to 1 st before m, k1, work next row of right cable patt to end.

Cont as est until Rows 1-12 of patts have been worked a total of 6 (7) times, then work Row 1 one more time.

Ribbed cuff is picked up and knitted after all dropped stitches have been unraveled.

Separate front and back

Next row: (WS) Work Row 2 of left cable patt to 1 st before m, m1, drop next st off needle, remove m, join a new ball of yarn, m1, work Row 2 of right cable patt to end—58 (71) sts each for front and back.

Next row: Work next row of right cable patt to 1 st before neck edge, k1; on other neck edge, k1, work next row of left cable patt to end.

Next row: Work left cable patt to 1 st before neck edge, p1; then p1, work right cable patt to end.

Cont as est, working Rows 5-12 of patts, then rep Rows 1-12 three more times, then work Rows 1-11 one more time.

Join front and back

Next row: (WS) Work in left cable patt as est to 2 sts before neck edge, p2tog, yo2, pm; then continuing with same yarn, ssp, work rem sts in right cable patt as est—115 (141) sts. Cut yarn at neck edge.

Next row: Work Row 1 of right cable patt to m, p1 in first yo, drop second yo, work Row 1 of left cable patt to end.

Next row: Work next row of left cable patt to 1 st before m, k1, work next row of right cable patt to end.

Cont as est, working Rows 3-12 of patts, then rep Rows 1-12; 5 (6) more times, then work Rows 1 and 2 one more time.

Begin drop stitches

Next row: (RS) K2, p1, *drop the next purl st, then (k1, p1, k1) into the top running thread, k2tog, yo, k8, yo, ssk; rep from * to last 6 sts, removing marker, drop the next purl st, then (k1, p1, k1) into the top running thread, k2tog, yo, p1, k2—133 (163) sts.

Next row: BO 3 sts knitwise, then bind off purlwise to last 3 sts, BO 1 st knitwise, k2tog, BO last st.

FINISHING

Draw each dropped stitch open so that it drops all the way to the end.
Weave in ends. Wet block poncho to finished measurements.

Cuff trim

With CO edge laying flat, place a locking stitch marker at each of the points indicated on schematic.

With smaller double-pointed needles, RS facing, and beg at first m, pick up and knit 40 (48) sts evenly to next m (approx 1 st in each CO st). Pm and join to work in the rnd.

First rnd: *K2, p2; rep from * to end.

Cont in rib for 2" [5 cm].

Next rnd: Bind off in pattern.

Repeat for BO edge.

Weave in ends and block again, if you like.

Dropped stitches make open ladders between cable panels. Wide neck is a simple slit.

Spate

Simple shapes are often the most versatile to wear. Spate is a long, narrow triangle that starts wide on one side edge and tapers to a narrow end on the other. Spate can be worn as an oversized kerchief or a shoulder-warming shawl. I'm sure you can come up with more configurations as well. Because the yarn makes such amazing twisted fringe, I couldn't resist adding long strands of it profusely along the cast on edge. Try adding beads above the knot for even more swing and bohemian appeal.

FINISHED MEASUREMENTS
24" [61 cm] wide and 48" [122 cm] long, before fringe

YARN
Sparrow by Quince & Co
(100% organic linen; 168yd [155m]/50g)
3 skeins Port 207

NEEDLES
One pair in size US 4 [3.5 mm]
Or size to obtain gauge

NOTIONS
Stitch markers
Crochet hook in size B [2.25 mm] or
C [2.75 mm]
Tapestry needle

GAUGE
22 sts and 32 rows = 4" [10 cm]
in stockinette stitch, after wet blocking.

CONSTRUCTION NOTES
Spate begins on a straight edge, as if you were to knit a rectangle. From there, decreases along the left edge of the rectangle morph the square shape into a triangle that tapers quickly at first and then more gradually to a blunt point.

STITCH PATTERNS
Right side panel (13 stitches)
Row 1: (RS) K1, k2tog, yo, k1-tbl, yo, ssk, k1, k2tog, yo, p1, k2tog, yo, k1.
Row 2: P3, (k1, p2) two times, p1-tbl, p2, k1.
Repeat Rows 1 and 2 for right side panel.

Left side panel (6 stitches)
Row 1: (RS) K2tog, yo, k1-tbl, yo, ssk, k1.
Row 2: K1, p2, p1-tbl, p2.
Repeat Rows 1 and 2 for left side panel.

KERCHIEF
Begin at wide end of kerchief
Using the long-tail cast on, CO 128 sts.
First row *place markers*: (WS) K6, place marker (pm), knit to last 13 sts, pm, knit to end.

Begin decreases
Next row *dec row*: (RS) Work Row 1 of right side panel to marker (m), slip marker (sl m), knit to 2 sts before next m, ssk, sl m, work Row 1 of left side panel to end (1 st dec'd)—127 sts rem.
Next row: Work Row 2 of left side panel to m, sl m, purl to next m, sl m, work Row 2 of right side panel to end.
Rep *dec row* every RS row 65 more times—62 sts rem.
Work 1 WS row.
Next row: (RS) Work right side panel to m, sl m, knit to next m, sl m, work left side panel to end.
Work 1 WS row.

Next row: Rep *dec row*—61 sts rem.

Rep *dec row* every 4 rows 5 more times, then every 6 rows 36 times—20 sts rem.

Work 5 rows even, removing markers on final row.

Next row *dec row*: (RS) K1, k2tog, yo, k1-tbl, yo, ssk, k1, k2tog, drop the next purl st from needle, then (k1, yo, k1, yo, k1) into top running thread of dropped st, k2tog, yo, ssk, k2tog, yo, k1-tbl, yo, ssk, k1. Unravel dropped st until it reaches CO edge.

Next row: Bind off knitwise.

FINISHING

Weave in ends. Wet block kerchief to finished measurements.

Add twisted fringe to CO edge.

TWISTED FRINGE

See page 14 for general fringe instructions.

Cut 132 strands in 19" [48.5 cm] lengths.

TIP: Work in four batches of 33 strands each. Wrap yarn around a 9" [23 cm] tall hardcover book or piece of sturdy cardboard 33 times, then cut at one end.

Secure a three-strand fringe into the right-hand corner of CO edge, then into every 3rd stitch along CO edge until you reach left-hand corner—44 pieces of fringe attached. Twist each fringe piece.

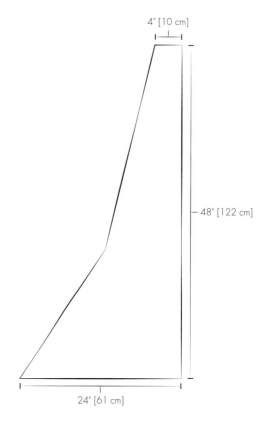

4" [10 cm]

48" [122 cm]

24" [61 cm]

A yarn-over eyelet pattern runs along the straight edge of the kerchief. A narrow variation of the eyelet pattern follows the shaped side.

Cella

This easy-going cardigan/shrug is worked as a rectangular piece then folded, origami style, to create sleeve openings. The ribbed border stabilizes the otherwise ethereal knitted fabric. And short rows widen the border near the bottom edge. Alternating rows of Sparrow and Kestrel add subtle color interest to the textured stitch pattern.

FINISHED MEASUREMENTS

32½ (37¼, 42¼, 47)"
[82.5 (94.5, 107.5, 119.5) cm] back width;
to fit approx 32-38 (38-44, 44-50, 50-56)"
[81.5-96.5 (96.5-112, 112-127, 127-142) cm] bust;
shown in size 32½" [82.5 cm]
on a 34" [86.5 cm] model

YARN

Kestrel by Quince & Co
(100% organic linen; 76yd [70m]/50g)
4 (8, 9, 11) skeins Anemone 513 (A)
and

Sparrow by Quince & Co
(100% organic linen; 168yd 5m]/50g)
2 (4, 5, 6) skeins Pink Grapefruit 217 (B)

NEEDLES

One 32" circular needle (circ)
in size US 9 [5.5 mm]
One 32" circ in size US 7 [4.5 mm]
Or size to obtain gauge

NOTIONS

Locking stitch markers
Waste yarn
Tapestry needle

GAUGE

15 sts and 16 rows = 4" [10 cm]
in stitch pattern with larger needles,
after wet blocking.

CONSTRUCTION NOTES

Shrug is worked flat, in one piece, from the bottom up in a stitch pattern alternating rows of Sparrow and Kestrel. The last row is bound off for blocking. For right and left ribbed borders, stitches are picked up along lower edges of rectangle, then bound-off stitches at neck edge are unraveled to center back and added to needle.

Border is worked in Kestrel only, one side of body at a time, with short row shaping. If between sizes and unsure which size to make, size down.

Stitch pattern

Texture pattern (multiple of 3 stitches + 2)

Row 1: (RS) With A and B held tog, k1, drop A to WS of work, with B, k1, *yo, k2; rep from * to end.

Row 2: *P2, drop yo from LH needle; rep from * to last 2 sts, p2.

Row 3: With A and B held tog, p1, drop B to WS of work, with A, purl to end.

Row 4: P1, *(p3tog, yo, p3tog) in next 3 sts; rep from * to last st, p1.

Repeat Rows 1-4 for texture pattern.

TECHNIQUES

yo short rows (see page 29 for detailed instructions)
(WS) With yarn behind RH needle, purl the next stitch. The yarn travels over the RH needle to purl, creating an extra stitch.
(RS) With yarn in front of RH needle, knit the next stitch. The yarn travels over the RH needle to knit, creating an extra stitch.

SHRUG

Begin at bottom edge

With A and larger circular needle (circ), using the long-tail cast on, CO 122 (140, 158, 176) sts. Do not join.

First row: (WS) Purl.

Begin stitch pattern

Next row: (RS) Work Row 1 of texture pattern to end.

Cont in patt until Rows 1-4 have been worked a total of 24 (25, 26, 27) times, then work Rows 1-3 one more time.

Piece meas approx 25 (26, 27, 28)" [63.5 (66, 68.5, 71) cm] when stretched to match blocked row gauge.

Next row: (RS) With A, bind off purlwise.

Weave in all ends except for bind off. Wet block shrug to finished measurements.

Measure up from CO edge 12 (12½, 13, 13½)" [30.5 (32, 33, 34.5) cm] along each side edge and place locking stitch markers.

RIGHT FRONT BORDER

With A and RS facing, using smaller circ, beg at lower edge of right front, pick up and knit 46 (49, 52, 55) sts evenly along side edge to marker. Carefully unravel bound off edge and place first 61 (70, 79, 88) sts onto LH needle, place rem 61 (70, 79, 88) sts onto waste yarn for left front, knit to end—107 (119, 131, 143) sts on needle.

First row: (WS) *P2, k2; rep from * to last 3 sts, p3.

A rectangle folded over on one end forms Cella's swingy body. Stitches picked up along the edge for the ribbed border secure the folded shape.

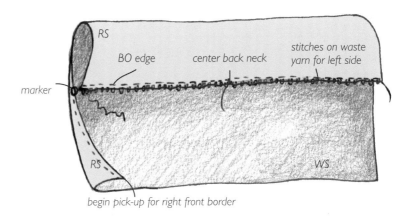

begin pick-up for right front border

HOW TO WORK YO SHORT ROWS IN STOCKINETTE STITCH

On the *right* side, work as established in your pattern to the point where the short row begins. Turn work.

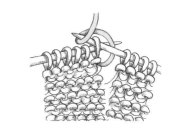

Fig 1

Now, with the wrong side facing, bring yarn to the back between the needles and purl the next stitch so that yarn travels up and over the RH needle, creating a yarnover next to the stitch just worked. (Fig 1) Still on wrong side, work in patt to the end of the row.

On the *wrong* side, work as established in your pattern to the point where the short row begins. Turn work.

Fig 2

With the right side facing, bring yarn to the front between the needles and knit the next stitch so that yarn travels up and over the RH needle, creating a yarnover next to the stitch just worked. (Fig 2) Still on right side, work as established to end of row.

When short rows are completed, resume working in established pattern. When you come to a yarnover, just before the gap created at the short-row turn (Figs 3 and 4), work the yarnover with the adjacent stitch as follows:

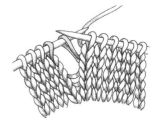

Fig 3

(RS) To work a *knit* stitch, k2tog (knit two stitches together, the yarnover with the next stitch) to close the gap.

(WS) To work a *purl* stitch, ssp (slip two stitches knitwise one at a time and purl them together through the back loops) to close the gap.

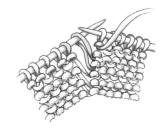

Fig 4

(WS) To work a *knit* stitch, ssk (slip two stitches knitwise one at a time and knit them together through the back loops) to close the gap.

(RS) To work a *purl* stitch, p2tog (purl two stitches together) to close the gap.

Note: Illustrations show technique in stockinette stitch. For Cella, work the short row yarnovers in ribbing as designated in pattern.

Begin short row shaping

Next row *short row 1*: (RS) K3, *p2, k2; rep from * to last 20 (24, 28, 32) sts, turn; (WS) yo, *p2, k2; rep from * to last 3 sts, p3.

Next row *short row 2*: (RS) Work in rib to 8 sts before last yo, turn; (WS) yo, work in rib to end.

Rep *short row two* 9 (10, 11, 12) more times—7 sts rem after last yo.

Next row: (RS) Work in rib to end, as you reach each yo, p2tog with the next st.

Next row: Bind off in pattern.

LEFT FRONT BORDER

Place sts held for left front onto smaller circ. Join yarn, ready to work a RS row.

First row: Knit to end, then beg at marker on left front, pick up and knit 46 (49, 52, 55) sts evenly along side edge to end—107 (119, 131, 143) sts on needle.

Next row: P3, *k2, p2; rep from * to end.

Next row: *K2, p2; rep from * to last st, p1.

Begin short row shaping

Next row *short row 1*: (WS) P3, *k2, p2; rep from * to last 20 (24, 28, 32) sts, turn; (RS) yo, *k2, p2; rep from * to last 3 sts, p3.

Next row *short row 2*: (WS) Work in rib to 8 sts before last yo, turn; (RS) yo, work in rib to end.

Rep *short row two* 9 (10, 11, 12) more times—7 sts rem after last yo.

Next row: (WS) Work in rib to end; as you reach each yo, ssk with the next st.

Next row: Bind off in pattern.

FINISHING

Sew together side edges of right and left trim at back neck.

Weave in remaining ends and block again, if you like.

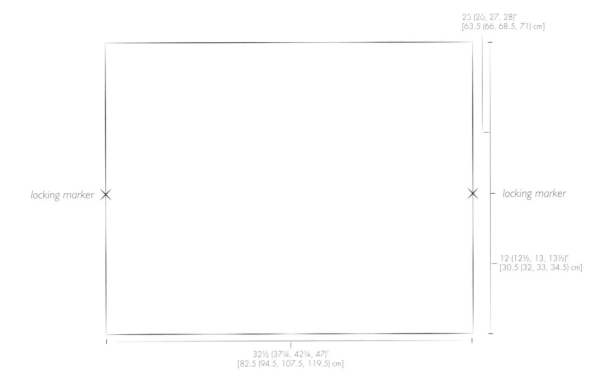

25 (26, 27, 28)"
[63.5 (66, 68.5, 71) cm]

locking marker ✕   ✕ — *locking marker*

12 (12½, 13, 13½)"
[30.5 (32, 33, 34.5) cm]

32½ (37¼, 42¼, 47)"
[82.5 (94.5, 107.5, 119.5) cm]

Arena

Arena is an oversized, boxy cardigan with pretty eyelet details and stitches that change direction. Knitted from the top down, the back yoke is picked up along side edges of a center column and knitted outward to the sleeves. The center fronts fan out gracefully, providing swing and lovely drape. Not quite seamless, Arena is a bit of a hybrid, combining circular- and flat-construction philosophies.

FINISHED MEASUREMENTS

40¼ (44, 47, 49¾, 53½, 56¼, 60¾, 63¾)"
[102 (112, 119.5, 126.5, 136, 143, 154.5, 162) cm] bust circumference; shown in size 47" [119.5 cm] with 13" [33 cm] positive ease

YARN

Sparrow by Quince & Co
(100% organic linen; 168yd [155m]/50g)
6 (6, 7, 8, 8, 9, 10, 11) skeins Port 207

NEEDLES

One pair or one 24" circular needle in size US 5 [3.75 mm]
Or size to obtain gauge

NOTIONS

Stitch markers
Waste yarn
Tapestry needle

GAUGE

22 sts and 28 rows = 4" [10 cm]
in stockinette stitch, after wet blocking.

CONSTRUCTION NOTES

Cardi begins with a narrow eyelet column at center back yoke. For right and left yokes, stitches are picked up along side edges of eyelet column and worked outward for yokes and neck trim, then continued to top of sleeve. (See illustrations on page 36.)

Back is picked up along lower edges of left and right yoke, with held center-column stitches between, and worked to hem.

Sleeves are picked up along side edges of back and front yoke, with held shoulder stitches between, and worked flat to cuff.

Sides and sleeves are seamed using the mattress stitch.

Entire piece can be worked with straight needles, but larger sizes may need a circular needle for back, to accommodate the large number of stitches.

SPECIAL ABBREVIATIONS

sl : Slip specified number of stitches purlwise with yarn to the WS of work.

CARDI

Begin center-back column at neck edge
Using the long-tail cast on, CO 9 sts.
First row: (WS) Knit.
Next row: Purl.
Next row: (WS) P3, k3, p3.
Next row: K1, k2tog, yo, k3, yo, ssk, k1.
Rep the last 2 rows until pc meas 4½ (5, 5, 5, 5½, 5½, 5½, 6)" [11.5 (12.5, 12.5, 12.5, 14, 14, 14, 15) cm] from beg, ending after a WS row.
Cut yarn. Place sts onto waste yarn. (See Fig 1, page 36.)

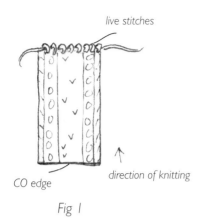

live stitches

direction of knitting

CO edge

Fig 1

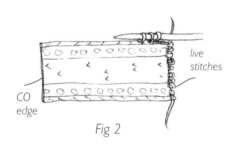

live stitches

CO edge

Fig 2

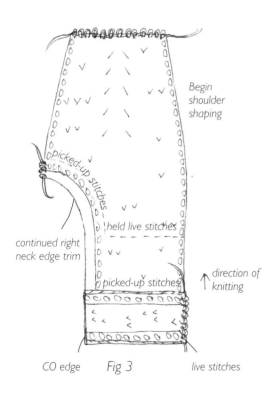

Begin shoulder shaping

Picked-up stitches

held live stitches

continued right neck edge trim

picked-up stitches

direction of knitting

CO edge *Fig 3* live stitches

Begin right back yoke

TIP: Gently steam to unroll side edges before picking up stitches.

With RS facing and live sts to the right and CO edge to the left, pick up and knit 24 (27, 27, 27, 30, 30, 30, 32) sts along top edge of piece (approx 3 sts for every 4 rows). (Fig 2)

First row: (WS) Sl 2 (neck edge), k5, purl to end.

Next row: K1, k2tog, yo, knit to last 9 sts, k2tog, yo, k7.

Cont as est until pc meas 2¼ (2½, 2½, 2½, 2¾, 2¾, 2¾, 3)" [5.5 (6.5, 6.5, 6.5, 7, 7, 7, 7.5) cm] from pick-up, ending after a RS row.

Next row *inc row*: (WS) Sl 2, k5, p1, p1-f/b, then place rem 15 (18, 18, 18, 21, 21, 21, 23) sts onto waste yarn (1 st inc'd)—10 sts on needle.

Continue right neck edge trim

Next row: (RS) K1, k2tog, yo, knit to end.

Next row: Sl 2, k5, purl to end.

Cont as est until neck trim meas 3 (3½, 3½, 3½, 4, 4, 4, 4½)" [7.5 (9, 9, 9, 10, 10, 10, 11.5) cm] from end of back yoke, ending after a WS row.

Cut yarn. Place sts onto waste yarn.

Continue right shoulder

Return sts held for right back yoke to needle, place marker (pm), then pick up and knit 15 (18, 18, 18, 21, 21, 21, 23) sts along edge of neck trim (approx 3 sts for every 4 rows)—30 (36, 36, 36, 42, 42, 42, 46) sts on needle. (Fig 3)

Next row: (WS) Purl.

Next row: K1, k2tog, yo, knit to last 3 sts, yo, ssk, k1.

Work 3 rows as est.

Begin shoulder shaping

Next row *dec row*: (RS) K1, k2tog, yo, knit to 3 sts before marker (m), ssk, k1, slip marker (sl m), k1, k2tog, knit to last 3 sts, yo, ssk, k1 (2 sts dec'd)—28 (34, 34, 34, 40, 40, 40, 44) sts rem.

Rep *dec row* every 6 rows 6 (2, 5, 8, 4, 7, 10, 8) more times, then every 4 rows 2 (9, 6, 3, 10, 7, 4, 8) times—12 sts rem.

Work 3 rows even, ending after a WS row.

Piece meas approx 7½ (8¼, 9, 9¾, 10½, 11¼, 12¼, 12¾)" [19 (21, 23, 25, 26.5, 28.5, 31, 32.5) cm] from last pick-up, 9¾ (10¾, 11½, 12¼, 13¼, 14, 15, 15¾)" [25 (27.5, 29, 31, 33.5, 35.5, 38, 40) cm] from pick-up at center back yoke.

Place sts onto waste yarn. Do not cut yarn.

RIGHT FRONT

With RS facing and attached yarn, pick up and knit 37 (40, 44, 48, 51, 55, 60, 62) sts along front side of shoulder edge (approx 2 sts for every 3 rows), return sts held for neck trim to LH needle, slip last picked-up st to LH needle, k2tog, then k2tog, yo, knit to end—46 (49, 53, 57, 60, 64, 69, 71) sts on needle.

Next row: (WS) Sl 2, k5, purl to end.

Next row: Knit to last 9 sts, k2tog, yo, k7.

Work 3 more rows as est.

Begin center front shaping

Next row *inc row*: (RS) Knit to last 7 sts, yo, k7 (1 st inc'd)—47 (50, 54, 58, 61, 65, 70, 72) sts.

Rep *inc row* every 6 rows 24 (25, 26, 27, 28, 29, 30, 31) more times—71 (75, 80, 85, 89, 94, 100, 103) sts.

Work 2 rows even.

Next row: (WS) Bind off knitwise.

Begin left back yoke

With RS facing, pick up and knit 24 (27, 27, 27, 30, 30, 30, 32) sts along side edge of center back yoke (approx 3 sts for every 4 rows).

Next row: (WS) Purl to last 7 sts, k5, p2.

Next row: Sl 2 (neck edge), k5, yo, ssk, knit to last 3 sts, yo, ssk, k1.

Cont as est until pc meas 2¼ (2½, 2½, 2½, 2¾, 2¾, 2¾, 3)" [5.5 (6.5, 6.5, 6.5, 7, 7, 7, 7.5) cm] from pick-up, ending after a RS row.

Next row: (WS) P15 (18, 18, 18, 21, 21, 21, 23) sts, then place these sts onto waste yarn, p1-f/b, p1, k5, p2 (1 st inc'd)—10 sts.

Continue left neck edge trim

Next row: (RS) Sl 2 (neck edge), k5, yo, ssk, k1.

Next row: P3, k5, p2.

Cont as est until neck trim meas 3 (3½, 3½, 3½, 4, 4, 4, 4½)" [7.5 (9, 9, 9, 10, 10, 10, 11.5) cm] from end of back yoke, ending after a WS row.

Place sts onto waste yarn. Do not cut yarn.

Continue left shoulder

With RS facing and held trim sts to the right, pick up and knit 15 (18, 18, 18, 21, 21, 21, 23) sts along side edge of trim, pm, return sts held for left back yoke to LH needle and knit across—30 (36, 36, 36, 42, 42, 42, 46) sts on needle.

Next row: (WS) Purl.

Next row: K1, k2tog, yo, knit to last 3 sts, yo, ssk, k1.

Work 3 rows as est.

Begin shoulder shaping

Next row *dec row*: (RS) K1, k2tog, yo, knit to 3 sts before m, ssk, k1, sl m, k1, k2tog, knit to last 3 sts, yo, ssk, k1 (2 sts dec'd)—28 (34, 34, 34, 40, 40, 40, 44) sts rem.
Rep *dec row* every 6 rows 6 (2, 5, 8, 4, 7, 10, 8) more times, then every 4 rows 2 (9, 6, 3, 10, 7, 4, 8) times—12 sts rem.
Work 3 rows even, ending after a WS row.
Piece meas approx 7½ (8¼, 9, 9¾, 10½, 11¼, 12¼, 12¾)" [19 (21, 23, 25, 26.5, 28.5, 31, 32.5) cm] from last pick-up, 9¾ (10¾, 11½, 12¼, 13¼, 14, 15, 15¾)" [25 (27.5, 29, 31, 33.5, 35.5, 38, 40) cm] from pick-up at center back yoke.
Place sts onto waste yarn. Do not cut yarn.

LEFT FRONT

Return sts held for trim to needle ready to work a RS row.
Next row: (RS) Sl 2, k5, yo, ssk, sl 1, pick up 1 st in side edge of left shoulder, return slipped st to LH needle, and k2tog, pick up and knit 37 (40, 44, 48, 51, 55, 60, 62) more sts along side edge—46 (49, 53, 57, 60, 64, 69, 71) sts on needle.
Next row: (WS) Purl to last 7 sts, k5, p2.
Next row: Sl 2, k5, yo, ssk, knit to end.
Work 3 more rows as est.

Begin center front shaping

Next row *inc row*: (RS) Sl 2, k5, yo, knit to end (1 st inc'd)—47 (50, 54, 58, 61, 65, 70, 72) sts.
Rep *inc row* every 6 rows 24 (25, 26, 27, 28, 29, 30, 31) more times—71 (75, 80, 85, 89, 94, 100, 103) sts.
Work 2 rows even.
Next row: (WS) Bind off knitwise.

BACK

With RS facing and beg at sts held for left shoulder, pick up and knit 53 (58, 62, 66, 71, 75, 81, 85) sts along side edge of left shoulder to held sts at center (approx 3 sts for every 4 rows), return held center sts to LH needle, slip last picked-up st to LH needle and k2tog, then pm, k2tog, yo, k3, yo, ssk, pm, sl 1, pick up 1 st in side edge of right shoulder, return slipped st to LH needle and k2tog, pick up and knit 52 (57, 61, 65, 70, 74, 80, 84) more sts along edge to held right shoulder sts—113 (123, 131, 139, 149, 157, 169, 177) sts on needle.
Next row: (WS) Purl to m, sl m, p2, k3, p2, sl m, purl to end.
Next row: Knit to m, sl m, k2tog, yo, k3, yo, ssk, sl m, knit to end.
Cont as est until back meas same as fronts, ending after a RS row.
Next row: (WS) Bind off knitwise.

Cardigan begins at neck with center back column. Left and right yoke are worked sideways to end of shoulder and lower back is worked down from yoke.

SLEEVE

Measure 4 (4¼, 4½, 4¾, 5, 5½, 5¾, 6)" [10 (11, 11.5, 12, 12.5, 14, 14.5, 15) cm] down from held shoulder sts and place locking st markers on front and back. With RS facing, pick up and knit 27 (29, 31, 33, 35, 37, 39, 41) sts from marker to held sts (approx 1 st in each row), return held sts to LH needle, slip last picked up st to LH needle and k2tog, then pm, k2tog, yo, k6, yo, ssk, pm, sl 1, pick up and knit 1 st in side edge, return slipped st to LH needle and k2tog, pick up and knit 26 (28, 30, 32, 34, 36, 38, 40) more sts to marker—64 (68, 72, 76, 80, 84, 88, 92) sts on needle.

Next row: (WS) Purl.
Next row: Knit to m, sl m, k2tog, yo, k6, yo, ssk, sl m, knit to end.
Next row: Purl.

Begin sleeve shaping

Next row *dec row*: (RS) Knit to 4 sts before m, ssk, k2, sl m, k2tog, yo, k6, yo, ssk, sl m, k2, k2tog, knit to end (2 sts dec'd)—62 (66, 70, 74, 78, 82, 86, 90) sts rem.
Rep *dec row* every 4 rows 7 (7, 7, 6, 6, 5, 5, 5) more times, then every RS row 0 (0, 0, 2, 2, 4, 4, 4) times—48 (52, 56, 58, 62, 64, 68, 72) sts rem.
Next row: (WS) Purl.
Next row: Knit.
Next row: Bind off knitwise.

FINISHING

Weave in ends. Wet block cardi to finished measurements.
Sew sleeve and side seams using the mattress stitch.

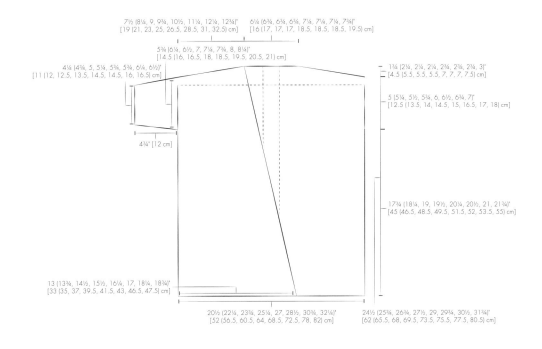

Detail of shoulder stitches continuing into sleeve.

Walkway

Walkway is a breezy shell, a lightweight layer to live in. Unassuming details give it interest. The textured panel, really two easy-to-knit panels alternating with each other, is set off-center and extends over the shoulder and down the back. The shoulders are shaped slightly to follow the body and a few increases extend them into short sleeves. The front's deep V-neck is echoed on the back with slanting eyelet columns.

FINISHED MEASUREMENTS

46¼ (49¼, 52, 55, 58, 60¾, 63¾, 66¾)"
[117.5 (125, 132, 139.5, 147.5, 154.5, 162, 169.5) cm] bust circumference; shown in size 49¼" [125 cm] with 15¼" [12.5 cm] positive ease

YARN

Sparrow by Quince & Co
(100% organic linen; 168yd [155m]/50g)
6 (7, 7, 8, 8, 9, 9, 9) skeins Penny 221

NEEDLES

One pair or one 24" circular needle in size US 5 [3.75 mm]
Or size to obtain gauge

NOTIONS

Stitch markers
Locking stitch markers
Waste yarn
Tapestry needle

GAUGE

22 sts and 28 rows = 4" [10 cm] in stockinette stitch, after wet blocking.

CONSTRUCTION NOTES

Shell front and back are worked separately from the bottom up. At the base of the V-neck, left and right front are separated and worked at the same time, with decreases worked well inside the center front edge to shape the neck, and increases near armhole edges to shape sleeve. Front and back panels are offset; they're placed on the left sides of front and back. Shoulders and sides are seamed. Entire piece can be worked with straight needles, but larger sizes may need a circular needle to accommodate the large number of stitches.

SPECIAL ABBREVIATIONS

sl 1: Slip 1 stitch purlwise with yarn to the WS of work.

STITCH PATTERNS

Center panel (29 stitches)
Row 1: (RS) *P2, sl 1, p1, sl 1, p6; rep from * one more time, p2, sl 1, p1, sl 1, p2.
Row 2: K2, p1, k1, p1, k2, *k6, p1, k1, p1, k2; rep from * one more time.
Row 3: *P2, sl 1, p1, sl 1, p2, (k1, yo) three times, k1; rep from * one more time, p2, sl 1, p1, sl 1, p2.
Row 4: K2, p1, k1, p1, k2, *(p1, drop the yo) three times, p1, k2, p1, k1, p1, k2; rep from * one more time.
Repeat Rows 1-4 for center panel.

Side panel (7 stitches)
Row 1: (RS) P2, sl 1, p1, sl 1, p2.
Row 2: K2, p1, k1, p1, k2.
Repeat Rows 1 and 2 for side panel.

SHELL

FRONT

Beg at bottom edge and using the long-tail cast on, CO 135 (143, 151, 159, 167, 175, 183, 191) sts.

First row *place markers*: (WS) P10, place marker for side panel (pm), p58 (62, 66, 70, 74, 78, 82, 86), pm for center panel, p29, pm for center panel, p28 (32, 36, 40, 44, 48, 52, 56), pm for side panel, p10 sts to end.

Begin stockinette and panels

Next row: (RS) K3, work Row 1 of side panel to marker (m), slip marker (sl m), knit to next m, sl m, work Row 1 of center panel to next m, sl m, knit to next m, work Row 1 of side panel to last 3 sts, k3.

Next row: P3, work side panel to m, sl m, purl to next m, sl m, work center panel to next m, sl m, purl to next m, work side panel to last 3 sts, p3.

Cont as est until pc meas 14" [35.5 cm] from beg, ending after a WS row.

Separate left and right front

Next row: (RS) K3, work side panel to m, sl m, knit to next m, work center panel to next m, k3, join a new ball of yarn and k28, pm for neck shaping, knit to next m, sl m, work side panel to last 3 sts, k3—70 (74, 78, 82, 86, 90, 94, 98) sts for left front and 65 (69, 73, 77, 81, 85, 89, 93) sts for right front.

Begin neck shaping

Next row: (WS) Work as est to first m, sl m, purl to right neck edge; on left neck edge p3, work center panel to next m, sl m, purl to last m, sl m, work as est to end. Work 2 rows even as est.

Next row *dec row*: (RS) Work as est to 4 sts before center panel m, ssk, k2, sl m, work as est to neck edge; then work to shaping m, sl m, k2tog, work as est to end (2 sts dec'd)—69 (73, 77, 81, 85, 89, 93, 97) sts rem for left front and 64 (68, 72, 76, 80, 84, 88, 92) sts for right.

Rep *dec row* every 4 rows 2 more times—67 (71, 75, 79, 83, 87, 91, 95) sts rem for left front and 62 (66, 70, 74, 78, 82, 86, 90) sts for right.

Work 3 rows even.

Place a locking stitch marker at the beg and end of last row for armhole placement.

Begin armhole shaping

Next row *inc/dec row*: (RS) Work to first m, sl m, M1L, knit to 4 sts before center panel m, ssk, k2, sl m, work to neck edge; then work to shaping m, sl m, k2tog, knit to last m, M1R, sl m, work to end (2 sts inc'd and 2 sts dec'd).

Rep *inc/dec row* every 4 rows 10 (11, 11, 12, 12, 13, 13, 14) more times. Work 3 rows even.

Begin shoulder shaping

Next row *dec row*: (RS) BO 4 (4, 4, 4, 5, 5, 6, 6) sts, work to 4 sts before center panel m, ssk, k2, sl m, work to neck edge; then work to shaping m, sl m, k2tog, work to end (2 sts dec'd).

Next row: BO 4 (4, 4, 4, 5, 5, 6, 6) sts, work to neck edge; then work to end— 62 (66, 70, 74, 77, 81, 84, 88) sts rem for left front and 57 (61, 65, 69, 72, 76, 79, 83) sts for right.

Next row: (RS) BO 4 (4, 4, 5, 5, 6, 6, 7) sts, work to neck edge; then work to end.

Next row: BO 4 (4, 4, 5, 5, 6, 6, 7) sts, work to neck edge; then work to end— 58 (62, 66, 69, 72, 75, 78, 81) sts rem for left front and 53 (57, 61, 64, 67, 70, 73, 76) sts for right.

Rep the last 2 rows 7 more times—30 (34, 38, 34, 37, 33, 36, 32) sts rem for left front and 25 (29, 33, 29, 32, 28, 31, 27) sts for right.

Next row: (RS) BO rem sts for right front; then work to end.

Next row: Bind off purlwise.

BACK

Beg at bottom edge and using the long-tail cast on, CO 135 (143, 151, 159, 167, 175, 183, 191) sts.

First row: (WS) P10, pm for side panel, p28 (32, 36, 40, 44, 48, 52, 56), pm for center panel, p29, pm for center panel, p58 (62, 66, 70, 74, 78, 82, 86), pm for side panel, p10 sts to end.

Begin stockinette and panels

Next row: (RS) K3, work Row 1 of side panel to m, sl m, knit to next m, sl m, work Row 1 of center panel to next m, sl m, knit to next m, work Row 1 of side panel to last 3 sts, k3.

Next row: P3, work side panel to m, sl m, purl to next m, sl m, work center panel to next m, sl m, purl to next m, work side panel to last 3 sts, p3.

Cont as est until pc meas same as front to separation for neck, ending after a WS row.

Begin back shaping

Next row *inc row*: (RS) K3, work side panel to first m, sl m, k27 (31, 35, 39, 43, 47, 51, 55), pm for shaping, k28, pm for back detail, yo, pm for detail, k3, sl m, work center panel to next m, sl m, knit to last m, work side panel to last 3 sts, k3 (1 st inc'd)—136 (144, 152, 160, 168, 176, 184, 192) sts.

Next row: Work to first m, sl m, purl to center panel m, sl m, work to next m, sl m, purl to last m, sl m, work to end.

Work 2 rows even as est.

Next row *inc/dec row*: (RS) Work to 2 sts before shaping m, ssk, sl m, knit to detail m, sl m, yo, knit to next detail m, yo, sl m, work to 2 sts past center panel, k2tog, work to end (2 sts inc'd and 2 sts dec'd).

Wide texture panel is really two different smaller panels that alternate. The wide panel is set off-center for more interest.

Rep *inc/dec row* every 4 rows 2 more times.
Work 3 rows even.
Place a locking stitch marker at the beg and end of last row for armhole placement.

Begin armhole shaping
Next row *inc row/dec row*: (RS) Work to first m, sl m, M1L, knit to 2 sts before shaping m, ssk, sl m, knit to detail m, sl m, yo, knit to next detail m, yo, sl m, work to 2 sts past center panel, k2tog, knit to last m, M1R, sl m, work to end (4 sts inc'd and 2 sts dec'd)—138 (146, 154, 162, 170, 178, 186, 194) sts.
Rep *inc row/dec row* every 4 rows 10 (11, 11, 12, 12, 13, 13, 14) more times—158 (168, 176, 186, 194, 204, 212, 222) sts.
Work 3 rows even.

Begin shoulder shaping
Next row *inc/dec row*: (RS) BO 4 (4, 4, 4, 5, 5, 6, 6) sts, work to 2 sts before shaping m, ssk, sl m, knit to detail m, sl m, yo, knit to next detail m, yo, sl m, work to 2 sts past center panel, k2tog, work to end.
Next row: BO 4 (4, 4, 4, 5, 5, 6, 6) sts, work to end—150 (160, 168, 178, 184, 194, 200, 210) sts rem.
Next row: (RS) BO 4 (4, 4, 5, 5, 6, 6, 7) sts, work to end.
Next row: BO 4 (4, 4, 5, 5, 6, 6, 7) sts, work to end—142 (152, 160, 168, 174, 182, 188, 196) sts rem.
Next row *inc row*: (RS) BO 4 (4, 4, 5, 5, 6, 6, 7) sts, work to detail m, sl m, yo, work to next detail m, yo, sl m, work to end (2 sts inc'd).
Next row: BO 4 (4, 4, 5, 5, 6, 6, 7) sts, work to end—136 (146, 154, 160, 166, 172, 178, 184) sts rem.
Rep the last 4 rows 2 more times—108 (118, 126, 124, 130, 128, 134, 132) sts rem.
Next row: (RS) BO 4 (4, 4, 5, 5, 6, 6, 7) sts, work to end.
Next row: BO 4 (4, 4, 5, 5, 6, 6, 7) sts, work to end—100 (110, 118, 114, 120, 116, 122, 118) sts rem.
Rep the last 2 rows 1 more time—92 (102, 110, 104, 110, 104, 110, 104) sts rem; 25 (29, 33, 29, 32, 28, 31, 27) sts for right shoulder, 30 (34, 38, 34, 37, 33, 36, 32) sts for left, and 37 (39, 39, 41, 41, 43, 43, 45) sts for back neck.
Next row: (RS) Bind off knitwise.

Sleeves are made by extending the shoulders.

FINISHING
Weave in ends. Wet block pieces to finished measurements.
Sew shoulder seams.
Sew side seams using the mattress stitch.

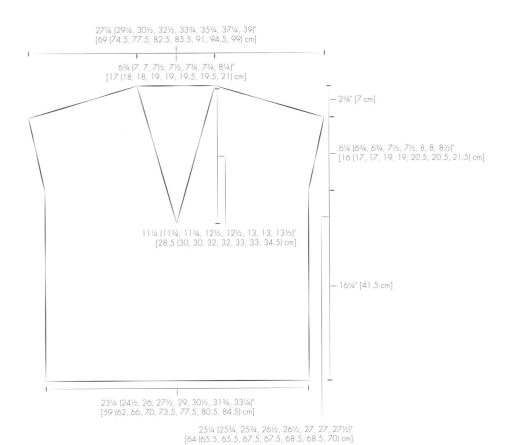

27¼ (29¼, 30½, 32½, 33¾, 35¾, 37¼, 39)"
[69 (74.5, 77.5, 82.5, 85.5, 91, 94.5, 99) cm]

6¾ (7, 7, 7½, 7½, 7¾, 7¾, 8¼)"
[17 (18, 18, 19, 19, 19.5, 19.5, 21) cm]

2¾" [7 cm]

6¼ (6¾, 6¾, 7½, 7½, 8, 8, 8½)"
[16 (17, 17, 19, 19, 20.5, 20.5, 21.5) cm]

11¼ (11¾, 11¾, 12½, 12½, 13, 13, 13½)"
[28.5 (30, 30, 32, 32, 33, 33, 34.5) cm]

16¼" [41.5 cm]

23¼ (24½, 26, 27½, 29, 30½, 31¾, 33¼)"
[59 (62, 66, 70, 73.5, 77.5, 80.5, 84.5) cm]

25¼ (25¾, 25¾, 26½, 26½, 27, 27, 27½)"
[64 (65.5, 65.5, 67.5, 67.5, 68.5, 68.5, 70) cm]

Bower

Bower is one long, slightly modified rectangle worked from the bottom edge of the fronts up over the shoulder and down the back. The curving edge of the oversized leaf motif becomes shaping for the neckline. Short sleeves are bumped out with increases on the front and bumped back in on the back. A two-slipped stitch edging knitted in as you go makes a smooth finish on the edge. An optional i-cord added across the back opening stabilizes the V-shaped back neckline. A single button works as a closure.

FINISHED MEASUREMENTS

35¼ (39½, 43¾, 48, 52¼, 56½)" [89.5 (100.5, 111, 122, 132.5, 143.5) cm] bust circumference; shown in size 39½" [100.5 cm] with 5½" [14 cm] positive ease

YARN

Kestrel by Quince & Co (100% organic linen; 76yd [70m]/50g) 6 (7, 8, 9, 10, 11) skeins Sand 501

NEEDLES

One pair or one 24" circular needle in size US 10 [6 mm]
One set double-pointed needles in size US 10 [6 mm]
Or size to obtain gauge

NOTIONS

Stitch markers
Waste yarn
Tapestry needle

GAUGE

15 sts and 20 rows = 4" [10 cm] in stockinette stitch, after wet blocking.

CONSTRUCTION NOTES

Cardigan begins at bottom edge of front pieces, which are worked separately up and over shoulders, then joined to work back to lower edge. Sides are seamed using the mattress stitch. A length of i-cord is attached at upper back for stability.

SPECIAL ABBREVIATIONS

sl 2: Slip 2 stitches purlwise with yarn to the WS of work.
m1-p/R (make 1 purlwise right slanting): Insert LH needle from back to front under horizontal strand between stitch just worked and next stitch, purl lifted strand through the front loop (1 stitch increased).
m1-p/L (make 1 purlwise left slanting): Insert LH needle from front to back under horizontal strand between stitch just worked and next stitch, purl lifted strand through the back loop (1 stitch increased).

STITCH PATTERNS

Right leaf (begins and ends as 16 stitches)

Row 1: (RS) Sl 2, p1, yo, k2, yo, p1, k2, p2tog, k6—17 sts.

Row 2: P6, k1, p2, k1, p4, k1, p2.

Row 3: Sl 2, p1, k1, yo, k2, yo, k1, p1, k2, p2tog, k5—18 sts.

Row 4: P5, k1, p2, k1, p6, k1, p2.

Row 5: Sl 2, p1, (k2, yo) two times, k2, p1, k2, p2tog, k4—19 sts.

Row 6: P4, k1, p2, k1, p8, k1, p2.

Row 7: Sl 2, p1, k3, yo, k2, yo, k3, p1, k2, p2tog, k3—20 sts.

Row 8: P3, k1, p2, k1, p10, k1, p2.

Row 9: Sl 2, p1, k4, yo, k2, yo, k4, p1, k2, p2tog, k2—21 sts.

Row 10: (P2, k1) two times, p12, k1, p2.

Row 11: Sl 2, p1, k5, yo, k2, yo, k5, p1, k2, p2tog, k1—22 sts.

Row 12: P1, k1, p2, k1, p14, k1, p2.

Row 13: Sl 2, p1, k6, yo, k2, yo, k6, p1, k2, p2tog—23 sts.

Row 14: K1, p2, k1, p6, k4, p6, k1, p2.

Row 15: Sl 2, yo, k2tog, k5, p1, k2, p1, k6, p1, k2, p1.

Row 16: Rep Row 14.

Row 17: Sl 2, p2tog, k5, p1, k2, p1, k5, ssp, k2, p1, M1L—22 sts rem.

Row 18: P1, k1, p2, k1, p5, k4, p5, k1, p2.

Row 19: Sl 2, p1, k5, p1, k2, p1, k5, p1, k2, p1, k1.

Row 20: Rep Row 18.

Row 21: Sl 2, p2tog, k4, p1, k2, p1, k4, ssp, k2, p1, M1L, k1—21 sts rem.

Row 22: (P2, k1) two times, p4, k4, p4, k1, p2.

Row 23: Sl 2, p1, k4, p1, k2, p1, k4, (p1, k2) two times.

Row 24: Rep Row 22.

Row 25: Sl 2, p2tog, k3, p1, k2, p1, k3, ssp, k2, p1, M1L, k2—20 sts rem.

Row 26: P3, k1, p2, k1, p3, k4, p3, k1, p2.

Row 27: Sl 2, (p1, k3, p1, k2) two times, p1, k3.

Row 28: Rep Row 26.

Row 29: Sl 2, p2tog, (k2, p1) two times, k2, ssp, k2, p1, M1L, k3—19 sts rem.

Row 30: P4, (k1, p2) two times, k4, p2, k1, p2.

Row 31: Sl 2, (p1, k2) four times, p1, k4.

Row 32: Rep Row 30.

Row 33: Sl 2, p2tog, k1, p1, k2, p1, k1, ssp, k2, p1, M1L, k4—18 sts rem.

Row 34: P5, k1, p2, k1, p1, k4, p1, k1, p2.

Row 35: Sl 2, (p1, k1, p1, k2) two times, p1, k5.

Row 36: Rep Row 34.

Row 37: Sl 2, p2tog, p1, k2, p1, ssp, k2, p1, M1L, k5—17 sts rem.

Row 38: P6, k1, p2, k6, p2.

Row 39: Sl 2, (p2, k2) two times, p1, k6.

Row 40: Rep Row 38.

Row 41: Sl 2, p2tog, k2, ssp, k2, p1, M1L, k6—16 sts rem.

Row 42: P7, k1, p2, k4, p2.

BOWER RIGHT LEAF

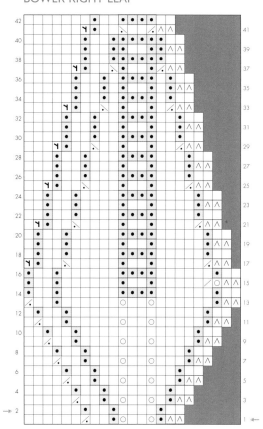

Left leaf (begins and ends as 16 stitches)

Row 1: (RS) K6, ssp, k2, p1, yo, k2, yo, p1, k2—17 sts.
Row 2: Sl 2, k1, p4, k1, p2, k1, p6.
Row 3: K5, ssp, k2, p1, k1, yo, k2, yo, k1, p1, k2—18 sts.
Row 4: Sl 2, k1, p6, k1, p2, k1, p5.
Row 5: K4, ssp, k2, p1, (k2, yo) two times, k2, p1, k2—19 sts.
Row 6: Sl 2, k1, p8, k1, p2, k1, p4.
Row 7: K3, ssp, k2, p1, k3, yo, k2, yo, k3, p1, k2—20 sts.
Row 8: Sl 2, k1, p10, k1, p2, k1, p3.
Row 9: K2, ssp, k2, p1, k4, yo, k2, yo, k4, p1, k2—21 sts.
Row 10: Sl 2, k1, p12, (k1, p2) two times.
Row 11: K1, ssp, k2, p1, k5, yo, k2, yo, k5, p1, k2—22 sts.
Row 12: Sl 2, k1, p14, k1, p2, k1, p1.
Row 13: Ssp, k2, p1, k6, yo, k2, yo, k6, p1, k2—23 sts.
Row 14: Sl 2, k1, p6, k4, p6, k1, p2, k1.
Row 15: P1, (k2, p1, k6, p1) two times, k2.
Row 16: Rep Row 14.
Row 17: M1R, p1, k2, p2tog, k5, p1, k2, p1, k5, ssp, k2—22 sts rem.
Row 18: Sl 2, k1, p5, k4, p5, k1, p2, k1, p1.
Row 19: K1, (p1, k2, p1, k5) two times, p1, k2.
Row 20: Rep Row 18.
Row 21: K1, M1R, p1, k2, p2tog, k4, p1, k2, p1, k4, ssp, k2—21 sts rem.
Row 22: Sl 2, k1, p4, k4, p4, (k1, p2) two times.
Row 23: (K2, p1) two times, k4, p1, k2, p1, k4, p1, k2.
Row 24: Rep Row 22.
Row 25: K2, M1R, p1, k2, p2tog, k3, p1, k2, p1, k3, ssp, k2—20 sts rem.
Row 26: Sl 2, k1, p3, k4, p3, k1, p2, k1, p3.
Row 27: (K3, p1, k2, p1) two times, k3, p1, k2.
Row 28: Rep Row 26.
Row 29: K3, M1R, p1, k2, p2tog, (k2, p1) two times, k2, ssp, k2—19 sts rem.
Row 30: Sl 2, k1, p2, k4, (p2, k1) two times, p4.
Row 31: K4, (p1, k2) five times.
Row 32: Rep Row 30.
Row 33: K4, M1R, p1, k2, p2tog, k1, p1, k2, p1, k1, ssp, k2—18 sts rem.
Row 34: Sl 2, k1, p1, k4, p1, k1, p2, k1, p5.
Row 35: K5, (p1, k2, p1, k1) two times, p1, k2.
Row 36: Rep Row 34.
Row 37: K5, M1R, p1, k2, p2tog, p1, k2, p1, ssp, k2—17 sts rem.
Row 38: Sl 2, k6, p2, k1, p6.
Row 39: K6, p1, (k2, p2) two times, k2.
Row 40: Rep Row 38.
Row 41: K6, M1R, p1, k2, p2tog, k2, ssp, k2—16 sts rem.
Row 42: Sl 2, k4, p2, k1, p7.

KEY

☐	knit on RS, purl on WS
•	purl on RS, knit on WS
○	yo
╱	k2tog
╱.	p2tog
╲.	ssp
r	M1R
Y	M1L
∧	sl 1
▨	no stitch

BOWER LEFT LEAF

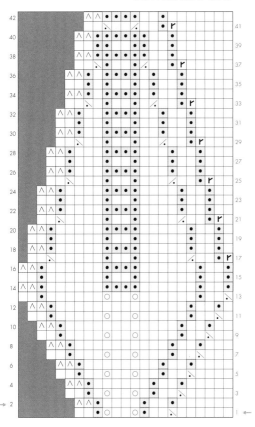

CARDIGAN

RIGHT FRONT

Beg at bottom edge and using the long-tail cast on, CO 28 (32, 36, 40, 44, 48) sts.

First row: (WS) Purl to last 9 sts, (k1, p2) three times to end.

Next row: Sl 2, (p1, k2) two times, p1, knit to end.

Cont as est until pc meas 4½ (4½, 5, 5, 5½, 5½)" [11.5 (11.5, 12.5, 12.5, 14, 14) cm] from beg, ending after a RS row.

Next row *place marker*: (WS) Purl to last 16 sts, place marker (pm) for leaf, work as est to end.

Begin right leaf

Next row: (RS) Work Row 1 of right leaf to marker (m), slip marker (sl m), knit to end.

Next row: Purl to m, sl m, work next row of right leaf to end.

Cont as est until leaf is complete, moving marker 7 sts closer to leaf edge on final row (marker is now 9 sts from center front edge).

Begin front sleeve shaping

Next row *RS inc row*: Sl 2, (p1, k2) two times, p1, sl m, knit to last 2 sts, M1R, k2 (1 st inc'd)—29 (33, 37, 41, 45, 49) sts.

Next row *WS inc row*: P2, m1-p/R, purl to m, sl m, k1, p2, k4, p2 (1 st inc'd)—30 (34, 38, 42, 46, 50) sts.

Rep the last 2 rows 4 more times—38 (42, 46, 50, 54, 58) sts.

Next row: (RS) Work as est to m, sl m, knit to end.

Next row: Using the knitted cast on, CO 3 sts, p2, k1, purl to m, sl m, work to end—41 (45, 49, 53, 57, 61) sts.

Work 4 (0, 2, 4, 0, 2) rows even.

Begin back neck shaping

Next row *inc row*: (RS) Work as est to m, sl m, M1L, knit to last 3 sts, p1, k2 (1 st inc'd)—42 (46, 50, 54, 58, 62) sts.

Rep *inc row* every 8 (10, 10, 10, 12, 12) rows 5 more times—47 (51, 55, 59, 63, 67) sts.

Work 12 (10, 12, 14, 12, 14) rows even, ending after a RS row.

Begin back sleeve shaping

Next row: (WS) BO 3 sts, purl to m, sl m, work as est to end—44 (48, 52, 56, 60, 64) sts rem.

Next row *RS dec row*: Work to m, sl m, knit to last 4 sts, ssk, k2 (1 st dec'd)—43 (47, 51, 55, 59, 63) sts rem.

Next row *WS dec row*: P2, p2tog, purl to m, sl m, work to end (1 st dec'd)—42 (46, 50, 54, 58, 62) sts rem.

Rep the last 2 rows 4 more times—34 (38, 42, 46, 50, 54) sts rem.

Cut yarn. Place sts onto waste yarn.

The oversized leaf motif provides a natural curve for the beginning of the neckline. A single button holds the two front pieces together.

LEFT FRONT

Beg at lower edge and using the long-tail cast on, CO 28 (32, 36, 40, 44, 48) sts.

First row: (WS) Sl 2, (k1, p2) two times, k1, purl to end.

Next row: Knit to last 9 sts, (p1, k2) three times to end.

Cont as est until pc meas 4½ (4½, 5, 5, 5½, 5½)" [11.5 (11.5, 12.5, 12.5, 14, 14) cm] from beg, ending after a RS row.

Next row *place marker*: (WS) Work as est for 16 sts, pm for leaf, purl to end.

Begin left leaf

Next row: (RS) Knit to m, sl m, work Row 1 of left leaf to end.

Next row: Work next row of left leaf to m, sl m, purl to end.

Cont as est until leaf is complete, moving marker 7 sts closer to leaf edge on final row (marker is now 9 sts from center front edge).

Begin front sleeve shaping

Next row *RS inc row*: K2, M1L, knit to m, sl m, (p1, k2) three times (1 st inc'd)—29 (33, 37, 41, 45, 49) sts.

Next row *WS inc row*: Sl 2, k4, p2, k1, sl m, purl to last 2 sts, m1-p/L, p2 (1 st inc'd)—30 (34, 38, 42, 46, 50) sts.

Rep the last 2 rows 4 more times—38 (42, 46, 50, 54, 58) sts.

Next row: (RS) Using the knitted cast on, CO 3 sts, k2, p1, knit to m, work as est to end—41 (45, 49, 53, 57, 61) sts.

Next row: Work to m, sl m, purl to last 3 sts, k1, p2.

Work 4 (0, 2, 4, 0, 2) rows even.

Begin back neck shaping

Next row *inc row*: (RS) K2, p1, knit to m, M1R, sl m, work as est to end (1 st inc'd)—42 (46, 50, 54, 58, 62) sts.

Rep *inc row* every 8 (10, 10, 10, 12, 12) rows 5 more times—47 (51, 55, 59, 63, 67) sts.

Work 11 (9, 11, 13, 11, 13) rows even, ending after a WS row.

Begin back sleeve shaping

Next row: (RS) BO 3 sts, knit to m, sl m, work as est to end—44 (48, 52, 56, 60, 64) sts rem.

Next row: Work to m, sl m, purl to end.

Next row *RS dec row*: K2, k2tog, knit to m, work to end (1 st dec'd)—43 (47, 51, 55, 59, 63) sts rem.

Next row *WS dec row*: Work to m, sl m, purl to last 4 sts, ssp, p2 (1 st dec'd)—42 (46, 50, 54, 58, 62) sts rem.

Rep the last 2 rows 4 more times—34 (38, 42, 46, 50, 54) sts rem.

A short length of i-cord stabilizes the deep V-shape of the back neck.

Join left and right pieces

Next row: (RS) Work across left front to last 2 sts, with RS facing, place first 2 sts of right front onto a double-pointed needle (dpn) and holding right front behind left front, knit the next st on left front tog with first st on dpn, then knit last left front st tog with rem st on dpn, return rem sts for right front to LH needle, (p1, k2) two times, p1, sl m, knit to end—66 (74, 82, 90, 98, 106) sts on needle.

Next row: (WS) Purl.

BACK

Next row: (RS) Knit.

Cont in St st until pc meas 12 (12, 12½, 12½, 13, 13)" [30.5 (30.5, 32, 32, 33, 33) cm] from joining row, ending after a WS row.

Next row: (RS) Bind off knitwise.

FINISHING

Weave in ends. Wet block cardigan to finished measurements.

Sew side seams using the mattress stitch.

I-cord

With dpns and using the long-tail cast on, CO 3 sts.

Next row: (RS) Work in i-cord as follows: *K3, do not turn, slide sts back to RH tip of needle; rep from * until i-cord meas 5" [12.5 cm] from beg.

Next row: Bind off knitwise.

Sew to right and left back neck edges, approx 6¾ (7, 7¼, 7½, 7¾, 8)" [17 (18, 18.5, 19, 19.5, 20.5) cm] up from back join.

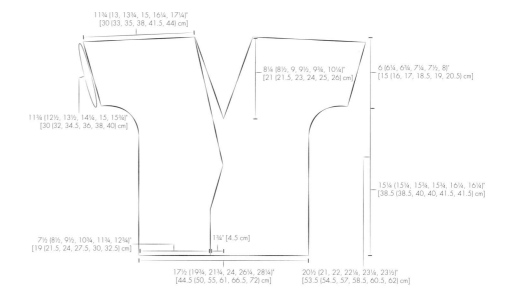

11¾ (13, 13¾, 15, 16¼, 17¼)"
[30 (33, 35, 38, 41.5, 44) cm]

8¼ (8½, 9, 9½, 9¾, 10¼)"
[21 (21.5, 23, 24, 25, 26) cm]

6 (6¼, 6¾, 7¼, 7½, 8)"
[15 (16, 17, 18.5, 19, 20.5) cm]

11¾ (12½, 13½, 14¼, 15, 15¾)"
[30 (32, 34.5, 36, 38, 40) cm]

15¼ (15¼, 15¾, 15¾, 16¼, 16¼)"
[38.5 (38.5, 40, 40, 41.5, 41.5) cm]

7½ (8½, 9½, 10¾, 11¾, 12¾)"
[19 (21.5, 24, 27.5, 30, 32.5) cm]

1¾" [4.5 cm]

17½ (19¾, 21¾, 24, 26¼, 28¼)"
[44.5 (50, 55, 61, 66.5, 72) cm]

20½ (21, 22, 22¼, 23¼, 23½)"
[53.5 (54.5, 57, 58.5, 60.5, 62) cm]

Two slipped stitches on the center front edges make a smooth, clean finish.

Arris

Although Arris may look complex, it's designed with the joy of the knitter in mind. Seaming is limited to sides and sleeves, and shoulders are joined using the three-needle bind off. Stitches are picked up along straight lines, no curves to contend with. Also, the pullover is reversible; wear it with the open V-neck in front and with the boatneck filled-in V in the back, or vice versa.

FINISHED MEASUREMENTS
32¾ (35¾, 39¼, 42¼, 45¾, 48¾)" [83 (91, 99.5, 107.5, 116, 124) cm] bust circumference; shown in size 32¾" [83 cm] with 1¼" [3 cm] negative ease

YARN
Sparrow by Quince & Co (100% organic linen; 168yd [155m]/50g) 5 (5, 6, 6, 7, 7) skeins Paprika 210

NEEDLES
One 24" circular needle (circ) in size US 4 [3.5 mm]
One spare needle in size US 4 [3.5 mm]
One 24" circ in size US 2 [2.75 mm]
Or size to obtain gauge

NOTIONS
Stitch markers
Waste yarn
Tapestry needle

GAUGE
22 sts and 33 rows = 4" [10 cm] in stockinette stitch with larger needles, after wet blocking.

CONSTRUCTION NOTES
Pullover is worked flat, in pieces, from the bottom up. It begins with a dropped-stitch hem followed by stockinette. Row-by-row decreases taper front and back pieces to a center point at the base of the V-neck. Stitches are then picked up along the diagonal eyelet columns for left and right yokes.

Front and back are worked identically, but for one of the sides (the back piece in the pattern), stitches are picked up along the edge of the neckline and worked in a mesh lace stitch to fill in the V. Stitches for sleeves are picked up along the armhole edge and worked flat, then seamed. Sides are seamed. Stitches are picked up around neck edge for a ribbed trim.

Although the mesh neckline is considered the back in the pattern, the sweater can be worn with it facing front or back.

SPECIAL ABBREVIATIONS
yo2 (yarn over twice / double yarnover): Bring yarn over needle twice.
s2kp (central double decrease): Slip 2 stitches tog knitwise to the RH needle, remove m, k1, pass 2 slipped stitches over knit stitch, replace m (2 stitches decreased).
s3k2p: Slip 3 stitches tog knitwise to RH needle, k2tog, pass slipped stitches over stitch created by k2tog (3 stitches decreased).

STITCH PATTERNS
Drop stitch pattern (begins as a multiple of 10 stitches)
Set up row 1: (RS) *K1, yo, ssk, k2tog, ssk, k2tog, yo, k1; rep from * to end (2 sts dec'd per repeat).
Set up row 2: *P2, p2tog, yo, ssp, p2; rep from * (1 st dec'd per repeat).
Row 1: *K1, yo, ssk, p1, k2tog, yo, k1; rep from *.
Row 2: *P3, k1, p3; rep from *.
Repeat Rows 1 and 2 for drop stitch pattern.

Eyelet panel (4 stitches)
Row 1: (RS) K2tog, yo2, ssk.
Row 2: P1, (p1, k1) in yo2, p1.
Repeat Rows 1 and 2 for eyelet panel.

PULLOVER

FRONT

Beg at bottom edge, with larger circular needle (circ) and using the long-tail cast on, CO 102 (110, 122, 130, 142, 150) sts. Do not join.

First row: (WS) Purl.

Begin drop stitch trim

Sizes 32¾ (-, 39¼, -, 45¾, -)" [83 (-, 99.5, -, 116, -) cm] only:

Next row: (RS) K1, work Set up row 1 of drop stitch pattern to last st, k1—82 (-, 98, -, 114, -) sts.

Next row: P1, work Set up row 2 of patt to last st, p1— 72 (-, 86, -, 100, -) sts.

Next row: K1, work Row 1 of patt to last st, k1.

Work 29 more rows as est, ending after Row 2 of patt.

Next row: (RS) K1, *k1, yo, ssk, drop next purl st from needle, yo, k2tog, yo, k1; rep from * to last st, k1.

Next row: P1, *p3, (p1, yo, p1) in yo, p3; rep from * to last st, p1; 20 (-, 24, -, 28, -) sts inc'd—92 (-, 110, -, 128, -) sts.

Proceed to **All sizes**.

Sizes - (35¾, -, 42¼, -, 48¾)" [- (91, -, 107.5, -, 124) cm] only:

Next row: (RS) K2, k2tog, yo, k1, work Set up row 1 of drop stitch pattern to last 5 sts, k1, yo, ssk, k2— - (90, -, 106, -, 122) sts.

Next row: P5, work Set up row 2 of patt to last 5 sts, p5— - (80, -, 94, -, 108) sts.

Next row: K2, k2tog, yo, k1, work Row 1 of patt to last 5 sts, k1, yo, ssk, k2.

Work 29 more rows as est, ending after Row 2 of patt.

Next row: (RS) K2, k2tog, yo, k1, *k1, yo, ssk, drop next purl st from needle, yo, k2tog, yo, k1; rep from * to last 5 sts, k1, yo, ssk, k2.

Next row: P5, *p3, (p1, yo, p1) in yo, p3; rep from * to last 5 sts, p5; - (20, -, 24, -, 28) sts inc'd— - (100, -, 118, -, 136) sts.

All sizes

Next row: (RS) Knit.

Piece meas approx 4¼" [11 cm] from beg.

Next row *place markers*: P42 (46, 51, 55, 60, 64), place marker (pm), p8, pm, p42 (46, 51, 55, 60, 64) sts to end.

Begin stockinette and center panel

Next row: (RS) Knit to marker (m), slip marker (sl m), work Row 1 of eyelet panel two times to next m, sl m, knit to end.

Next row: Purl to m, sl m, work eyelet panel to next m, sl m, purl to end.

Cont as est until pc meas 4½ (4, 3½, 5, 5, 5)" [11.5 (10, 9, 12.5, 12.5, 12.5) cm] from beg of St st, ending after a WS row.

Begin diagonal eyelet

Next row *dec row 1*: (RS) K1, ssk, yo, ssk, knit to m, sl m, work eyelet panel, sl m, knit to last 5 sts, k2tog, yo, k2tog, k1 (2 sts dec'd)—90 (98, 108, 116, 126, 134) sts rem.

Next row: Purl to m, sl m, work eyelet panel, sl m, purl to end.

Next row *dec row 2*: K1, ssk, yo, ssk, k2tog, knit to m, sl m, work eyelet panel, sl m, knit to last 7 sts, ssk, k2tog, yo, k2tog, k1 (4 sts dec'd)—86 (94, 104, 112, 122, 130) sts rem.

Next row: Purl to m, sl m, work eyelet panel, sl m, purl to end.

Sizes 32¾ (35¾, 39¼, -, -, -)" [83 (91, 99.5, -, -, -) cm] only:

Rep the last 4 rows 11 (12, 14, -, -, -) more times, then work *dec row 1* every RS row 1 (2, 1, -, -, -) more time(s)—18 sts rem.

Proceed to **All sizes**.

Size 42¼" [107.5 cm] only:

Next row: (RS) Rep *dec row 2*—108 sts rem.

Work 1 WS row.

Next row: Rep *dec row 1*—106 sts rem.

Work 1 WS row.

Next row: Work *dec row 2*—102 sts rem.

Work 1 WS row.

Rep the last 6 rows eight more times, then rep *dec row 2* one more time—18 sts rem.

Proceed to **All sizes**.

Sizes - (-, -, -, 45¾, 48¾)" [- (-, -, -, 116, 124) cm] only:

Next row: (RS) Rep *dec row 2*— - (-, -, -, 118, 126) sts rem.

Rep *dec row 2* every RS row - (-, -, -, 25, 27) more times—18 sts rem.

All sizes

Work 1 WS row, removing markers.

Next row *triple dec row*: (RS) K1, sssk, k3tog, yo2, k2tog, ssk, yo2, sssk, k3tog, k1 (6 sts dec'd)—12 sts rem.

Next row: P3, (p1, k1) in yo2, p2, (p1, k1) in yo2, p3.

Cut yarn.

Begin right front shoulder

With RS facing, slip the first 6 sts onto waste yarn for left front.

Next row: Join yarn as follows: Insert tip of LH needle from front to back under horizontal strand between held sts and first st on LH needle, knit lifted strand through the front loop, k2tog, yo2, ssk, pm, ssk, then pick up and knit 51 (57, 63, 61, 57, 61) sts along slanting, decreased edge (1 st in each row, skipping the first row)—57 (63, 69, 67, 63, 67) sts on needle.

Next row: Purl to m, sl m, p1, (p1, k1) in yo2, p2.

Arris worn with empty V in back.

Begin side-edge decreases

Sizes 32¾ (35¾, 39¼, 42¼, -, -)" [83 (91, 99.5, 107.5, -, -) cm] only:

Next row *dec row 1:* (RS) K1, work eyelet panel, sl m, knit to last 3 sts, ssk, k1 (1 st dec'd)—56 (62, 68, 66, -, -) sts rem.

Next row: Purl to m, sl m, work eyelet panel to last st, p1.

Next row *dec row 2:* (RS) K1, work eyelet panel, sl m, knit to last 5 sts, ssk two times, k1 (2 sts dec'd)—54 (60, 66, 64, -, -) sts rem.

Next row: Purl to m, sl m, work eyelet panel to last st, p1.

Rep the last 4 rows 4 (5, 6, 4, -, -) more times—42 (45, 48, 52, -, -) sts rem.
Proceed to **All sizes.**

Sizes - (-, -, -, 45¾, 48¾)" [- (-, -, -, 116, 124) cm] only:

Next row *dec row:* (RS) K1, work eyelet panel, sl m, knit to last 3 sts, ssk, k1 (1 st dec'd)— - (-, -, -, 62, 66) sts rem.

Rep *dec row* every 4 rows - (-, -, -, 7, 8) more times— - (-, -, -, 55, 58) sts rem.

All sizes

Work even as est until pc meas 5¼ (5½, 5¾, 6, 6¼, 6½)" [13.5 (14, 14.5, 15, 16, 16.5) cm] from final dec row, ending after a WS row.

Next row *eyelet row:* (RS) K1, work eyelet panel to m, sl m, *yo, k2tog; rep from * to last st, k1.

Next row: Purl to m, sl m, work eyelet panel to last st, p1.

Work 3 more rows in St st and eyelet panel, ending after a RS row.

Cut yarn, leaving a 24 (24, 28, 28, 32, 32)" [60 (60, 70, 70, 80, 80) cm] tail for finishing. Place sts onto waste yarn.

Begin left front shoulder

With RS facing and larger circ, beg at right side of dec edge, pick up and knit 51 (57, 63, 61, 57, 61) sts along dec edge (1 st in each row, skipping the last row), return 6 held sts to LH needle, k2tog, pm, k2tog, yo2, ssk, then insert tip of LH needle from front to back under same strand used for first shoulder, knit lifted strand through the front loop—57 (63, 69, 67, 63, 67) sts on needle.

Next row: P1, (p1, k1) in yo2, p2, sl m, purl to end.

Begin side-edge decreases

Sizes 32¾ (35¾, 39¼, 42¼, -, -)" [83 (91, 99.5, 107.5, -, -) cm] only:

Next row *dec row 1:* (RS) K1, k2tog, knit to m, sl m, work eyelet panel to last st, k1 (1 st dec'd)—56 (62, 68, 66, -, -) sts rem.

Next row: P1, work eyelet panel, sl m, purl to end.

Next row *dec row 2:* (RS) K1, k2tog two times, knit to m, sl m, work eyelet panel to last st, k1 (2 sts dec'd)—54 (60, 66, 64, -, -) sts rem.

Next row: P1, work eyelet panel, sl m, purl to end.

Rep the last 4 rows 4 (5, 6, 4, -, -) more times—42 (45, 48, 52, -, -) sts rem.
Proceed to **All sizes**.

Front and back are identical, but one of the pieces has the V-neck filled in with a knitted-in lace mesh.

Sizes - (-, -, -, -, 45¾, 48¾)" [- (-, -, -, 116, 124) cm] only:
Next row *dec row*: (RS) K1, k2tog, knit to m, sl m, work eyelet panel to last st, k1
(1 st dec'd)— - (-, -, -, 62, 66) sts rem.
Rep *dec row* every 4 rows - (-, -, -, 7, 8) more times— - (-, -, -, 55, 58) sts rem.

All sizes
Work even as est until pc meas 5¼ (5½, 5¾, 6, 6¼, 6½)" [13.5 (14, 14.5, 15, 16, 16.5) cm]
from final dec row, ending after a WS row.
Next row *eyelet row*: (RS) K1, *ssk, yo; rep from * to m, sl m, work eyelet panel to
last st, k1.
Next row: P1, work eyelet panel, sl m, purl to end.
Work 3 more rows in St st and eyelet panel, ending after a RS row.
Cut yarn, leaving a 24 (24, 28, 28, 32, 32)" [60 (60, 70, 70, 80, 80) cm] tail for finishing.
Place sts onto waste yarn.

BACK
Beg at lower edge, with larger circ and using the long-tail cast on, CO 102 (110, 122,
130, 142, 150) sts. Do not join.
Work Back same as for Front.

Begin mesh neckline
With RS facing and larger circ, beg at top of right shoulder, pick up and knit 42 (46,
40, 46, 44, 46) sts along neck edge to center; approx 2 sts for every 3 rows for sizes
32¾ (35¾, -, 42¼, -, -)" [83 (91, -, 107.5, -, -) cm] and approx 1 st for every 2 rows
for sizes - (-, 39¼, -, 45¾, 48¾)" [- (-, 99.5, -, 116, 124) cm], pick up and knit 1 st in
center, pm, then pick up and knit 42 (46, 40, 46, 44, 46) sts to top of left shoulder—
85 (93, 81, 93, 89, 93) sts on needle.
First row: (WS) Purl.
Next row *dec row*: (RS) K1, (k2tog, yo) to 4 sts before m, k2tog, s2kp, (ssk, yo) to last
3 sts, ssk, k1 (4 sts dec'd)—81 (89, 77, 89, 85, 89) sts rem.
Rep *dec row* every RS row 18 (20, 17, 20, 19, 20) more times—9 sts rem.
Next row: (WS) Purl.
Next row *dec row*: (RS) K1, k2tog, s2kp, ssk, k1 (4 sts dec'd)—5 sts rem.
Next row: Purl to end, removing marker.
Next row *dec row*: S3k2p (4 sts dec'd)—1 st rem.
Cut yarn and draw through remaining st.

Join shoulders
Return sts for left front and back shoulder to larger circ so that needle tips are at
armhole edge of each shoulder. With WS of pcs tog, attached yarn, and spare larger
needle, using the three-needle bind off, BO all sts. Rep for right shoulder.

Mesh filler makes a boat neck.

*Eyelet details along diagonal lines,
and top of shoulder.*

SLEEVE

With RS facing and larger circ, beg at end of side shaping, pick up and knit 72 (74, 76, 80, 82, 86) sts evenly along armhole edge to end of side shaping on other side (approx 3 sts for every 4 rows).

First row: (WS) P16 (17, 18, 20, 21, 23), pm, p40, pm, p16 (17, 18, 20, 21, 23) sts to end.

Begin stockinette and drop stitch panel

Next row: (RS) Knit to m, sl m, work Set up row 1 of drop stitch patt to next m, sl m, knit to end (8 sts dec'd)—64 (66, 68, 72, 74, 78) sts rem.

Next row: Purl to m, sl m, work Set up row 2 of patt to next m, sl m, purl to end (4 sts dec'd)—60 (62, 64, 68, 70, 74) sts rem.

Next row: Knit to m, sl m, work Row 1 of patt, sl m, knit to end.

Work 5 more rows as est.

Begin sleeve shaping

Next row *dec row*: (RS) K2, k2tog, work as est to last 4 sts, ssk, k2 (2 sts dec'd)—58 (60, 62, 66, 68, 72) sts rem.

Rep *dec row* every 8 (8, 8, 6, 6, 6) rows 6 (6, 6, 8, 8, 8) more times—46 (48, 50, 50, 52, 56) sts rem.

Sleeve meas approx 7" [18 cm] from pick-up.

Work 3 more rows as est.

Next row: (RS) Knit to m, sl m, *k1, yo, ssk, drop next purl st from needle, yo, k2tog, yo, k1; rep from * to m, sl m, knit to end.

Next row: Purl to m, sl m, *p3, (p1, yo, p1) in yo, p3; rep from * to m, sl m, purl to end (8 sts inc'd)—54 (56, 58, 58, 60, 64) sts.

Next row: Knit to end, removing markers.

Next row: (WS) Bind off knitwise.

FINISHING

Weave in ends. Wet block pullover to finished measurements.

Sew side and sleeve seams using the mattress stitch.

Neck trim

With RS facing and smaller circ, beg at center of back neck, pick up and knit 29 (32, 27, 29, 30, 32) sts along back neck to shoulder seam (approx 2 sts for every 3 rows), pick up and knit 48 (53, 58, 56, 63, 65) along front neck to center (approx 3 sts for every 4 rows), pick up and knit 1 st in center, pm, pick up and knit 48 (53, 58, 56, 63, 65) along front neck to shoulder seam, then pick up and knit 29 (32, 27, 29, 30, 32) sts along back neck to end—155 (171, 171, 171, 187, 195) sts on needle. Pm for beg of rnd.

First rnd: P1, (k2, p2) to 1 st before center front m, k1, sl m, (p2, k2) to last st, p1.

Next rnd *dec rnd*: Work in rib to 2 sts before m, s2kp, cont in rib to end (2 sts dec'd)—153 (169, 169, 169, 185, 193) sts rem.

Next rnd: Work in rib to 1 st before m, k1, sl m, work in rib to end.

Next rnd: Rep *dec rnd*—151 (167, 167, 167, 183, 191) sts rem.

Next rnd: Bind off in pattern.

Weave in remaining ends. Block again, if you like.

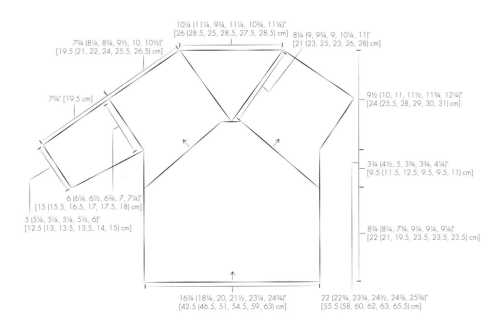

10¼ (11¼, 9¾, 11¼, 10¾, 11¼)" [26 (28.5, 25, 28.5, 27.5, 28.5) cm]

8¼ (9, 9¾, 9, 10¼, 11)" [21 (23, 25, 23, 26, 28) cm]

7¾ (8¼, 8¾, 9½, 10, 10½)" [19.5 (21, 22, 24, 25.5, 26.5) cm]

7¾" [19.5 cm]

9½ (10, 11, 11½, 11¾, 12¼)" [24 (25.5, 28, 29, 30, 31) cm]

3¾ (4½, 5, 3¾, 3¾, 4¼)" [9.5 (11.5, 12.5, 9.5, 9.5, 11) cm]

6 (6¼, 6½, 6¾, 7, 7¼)" [15 (15.5, 16.5, 17, 17.5, 18) cm]

5 (5¼, 5¼, 5¼, 5½, 6)" [12.5 (13, 13.5, 13.5, 14, 15) cm]

8¾ (8¼, 7¾, 9¼, 9¼, 9¼)" [22 (21, 19.5, 23.5, 23.5, 23.5) cm]

16¾ (18¼, 20, 21½, 23¼, 24¾)" [42.5 (46.5, 51, 54.5, 59, 63) cm]

22 (22¾, 23¾, 24½, 24¾, 25¾)" [55.5 (58, 60, 62, 63, 65.5) cm]

Annex

Annex is a tank top with rectangular inserts, called godets, knitted in at the same time as the body. The construction is unusual in that the body is knitted in one long piece, beginning at the front's lower edge and ending at the lower edge of the back. Eyelet columns in the center front and back and drapey dropped stitches on the godets make the piece open and airy.

FINISHED MEASUREMENTS
34 (37, 40, 43, 46, 49, 52, 55)"
[86.5 (94, 101.5, 109, 117, 124.5, 132, 139.5) cm] bust circumference; shown in size 34" [86.5 cm] with no ease

YARN
Kestrel by Quince & Co
(100% organic linen; 76yd [70m]/50g)
6 (6, 6, 7, 8, 8, 9, 10) skeins Sand 501

NEEDLES
One 32" circular needle
in size US 9 [5.5 mm]
Or size to obtain gauge

NOTIONS
Stitch markers
Waste yarn
Tapestry needle

GAUGE
16 sts and 22 rows = 4" [10 cm]
in stockinette stitch, after wet blocking.

CONSTRUCTION NOTES
Pullover is worked flat, from the bottom up, beginning with the front. Back continues down from the shoulder. Side panels (godets) at the hip are worked at the same time as front to top of hip, then godet stitches are placed on hold while continuing the upper body, armholes, and neck shaping on front and back. The side panels are rejoined when back piece is same length as front to godet stitches. Front and back pieces above the godet are joined with mattress stitch.

SPECIAL ABBREVIATION
sl 1: Slip 1 stitch purlwise with yarn to the WS of work.

STITCH PATTERNS
Center panel (14 stitches)
Row 1: (RS) P2, yo, p2tog, k6, p2, yo, p2tog.
Row 2: K2, yo, ssk, p6, k2, yo, ssk.
Repeat Rows 1 and 2 for center panel.

Side panel / godet (21 stitches)
Row 1: K4, p2, k1, yo, p2tog, k3, p2, k1, yo, p2tog, k4.
Row 2: P4, k2, p1, yo, ssk, p3, k2, p1, yo, ssk, p4.
Repeat Rows 1 and 2 for side panel.

TANK
FRONT
Beg at bottom edge and using the long-tail cast on, CO 62 (68, 74, 80, 86, 92, 98, 104) sts. Do not join.

Begin patterns
First row *place markers*: (RS) Work Row 1 of side panel over 21 sts (godet), p1, place marker (pm), k2 (5, 8, 11, 14, 17, 20, 23), pm, work Row 1 of center panel over 14 sts, pm, k2 (5, 8, 11, 14, 17, 20, 23), pm, p1, work Row 1 of side panel to end (godet).
Next row: Work next row of side panel to 1 st before marker (m), k1, slip marker (sl m), purl to next m, sl m, work next row of center panel to next m, sl m, purl to next m, sl m, k1, work next row of side panel to end.

Rectangular godet is knitted into angled opening of front and back body.

Begin side-body increases

Next row *inc row*: (RS) Work as est to m, sl m, M1L, knit to next m, sl m, work as est to next m, sl m, knit to next m, M1R, sl m, work as est to end (2 sts inc'd)—64 (70, 76, 82, 88, 94, 100, 106) sts.

Rep *inc row* every RS row 17 more times—98 (104, 110, 116, 122, 128, 134, 140) sts.

Next row *double inc row*: (RS) Work as est to m, sl m, M1L, k2, M1L, knit to next m, sl m, work to next m, sl m, knit to 2 sts before next m, M1R, k2, M1R, sl m, work to end (4 sts inc'd)—102 (108, 114, 120, 126, 132, 138, 144) sts.

Rep *double inc row* every RS row 2 more times—110 (116, 122, 128, 134, 140, 146, 152) sts.

Work 1 WS row.

Separate body and side panels

Next row: (RS) Work godet sts to 1 st before marker, then place these sts onto waste yarn, k1, remove m, work to last m, remove m, k1, then place rem 21 godet sts onto waste yarn—68 (74, 80, 86, 92, 98, 104, 110) sts on needle.

Next row: Purl to m, work center panel to next m, purl to end.

Cont as est in St st and center panel until pc meas 12¼ (12¼, 12¼, 12¾, 12¾, 13¼, 13¼, 13¾)" [31 (31, 31, 32.5, 32.5, 33.5, 33.5, 35) cm] from beg (measuring straight down at center), ending after a WS row.

Begin armhole shaping

Next row: (RS) Using the cable cast on, CO 3 sts, work as est to end.

Next row: Using the cable cast on, CO 3 sts, work as est to end—74 (80, 86, 92, 98, 104, 110, 116) sts.

Next row *double dec row*: (RS) K3, k2tog two times, work to last 7 sts, ssk two times, k3 (4 sts dec'd)—70 (76, 82, 88, 94, 100, 106, 112) sts rem.

Rep *double dec row* every RS row 4 (6, 7, 8, 8, 8, 8, 9) more times—54 (52, 54, 56, 62, 68, 74, 76) sts rem.

Work 1 WS row.

Next row *dec row*: (RS) K3, k2tog, knit to last 5 sts, ssk, k3 (2 sts dec'd)—52 (50, 52, 54, 60, 66, 72, 74) sts rem.

Rep *dec row* every RS row 4 (2, 2, 2, 3, 4, 6, 6) more times—44 (46, 48, 50, 54, 58, 60, 62) sts rem.

Work 1 WS row.

Begin neck shaping

Next row: (RS) Knit to m, remove m, join a new ball of yarn and BO all sts purlwise to next m, removing m to BO last st, knit to end—15 (16, 17, 18, 20, 22, 23, 24) sts rem for each side.

Next row: Purl to right neck edge; on left neck edge, purl to end.

Next row *double dec row*: (RS) Knit to 7 sts before neck edge, ssk two times, k3; then k3, k2tog two times, knit to end (2 sts dec'd at each neck edge)—13 (14, 15, 16, 18, 20, 21, 22) sts rem each.

Rep *double dec row* every RS row 1 (1, 2, 2, 3, 3, 4, 4) more times—11 (12, 11, 12, 12, 14, 13, 14) sts rem.

Work 1 WS row.

Next row *dec row*: (RS) Knit to 5 sts before neck edge, ssk, k3; then k3, k2tog, knit to end (1 st dec'd each neck edge)—10 (11, 10, 11, 11, 13, 12, 13) sts rem.

Rep *dec row* every RS row 2 (3, 2, 2, 2, 3, 2, 3) more times—8 (8, 8, 9, 9, 10, 10, 10) sts rem.

Cont in St st until pc meas 2" [5 cm] from final dec row, ending after a WS row. Back is now worked from the shoulders down.

BACK

Next row *double inc row*: (RS) Knit to 3 sts before neck edge, M1L, k1, M1L, k2; then k2, M1R, k1, M1R, knit to end (2 sts inc'd each neck edge)—10 (10, 10, 11, 11, 12, 12, 12) sts.

Rep *double inc row* every RS row 2 (2, 3, 3, 4, 4, 5, 5) more times—14 (14, 16, 17, 19, 20, 22, 22) sts.

Cast on for back neck and join right and left sides

Next row: (WS) Purl to neck edge, turn work, using the cable cast on, CO 17 (19, 17, 17, 17, 19, 17, 19) sts, turn work, k1 from second shoulder, pass the last CO st over this st, then purl to end—44 (46, 48, 50, 54, 58, 60, 62) sts on needle.

Begin center panel

Next row *place markers*: (RS) K15 (16, 17, 18, 20, 22, 23, 24), pm, work Row 1 of center panel over 14 sts, pm, knit to end.

Work as est in St st and center panel until pc meas 3 (3, 2¾, 2¾, 2¾, 2¾, 2½, 2½)" [7.5 (7.5, 7, 7, 7, 7, 6.5, 6.5) cm] from back neck CO, ending after a WS row.

Begin armhole shaping

Next row *inc row*: (RS) K3, M1L, work as est to last 3 sts, M1R, k3 (2 sts inc'd)—46 (48, 50, 52, 56, 60, 62, 64) sts.

Rep *inc row* every RS row 4 (2, 2, 2, 3, 4, 6, 6) more times—54 (52, 54, 56, 62, 68, 74, 76) sts.

Work 1 WS row.

Next row *double inc row*: (RS) K3, M1L, k1, M1L, work to last 4 sts, M1R, k1, M1R, k3 (4 sts inc'd)—58 (56, 58, 60, 66, 72, 78, 80) sts.

Rep *double inc row* every RS row 4 (6, 7, 8, 8, 8, 8, 9) more times—74 (80, 86, 92, 98, 104, 110, 116) sts.

Work 1 WS row.

Next row: (RS) BO 3 sts, work to end.

Next row: BO 3 sts, work to end—68 (74, 80, 86, 92, 98, 104, 110) sts rem.

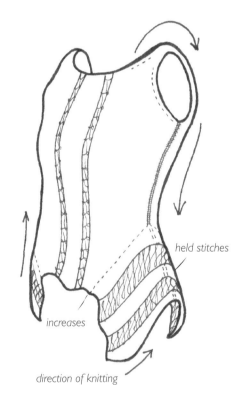

held stitches

increases

direction of knitting

Back body

Next row: (RS) Knit to m, work center panel to next m, knit to end.
Cont as est until pc meas 4½ (4½, 4½, 5, 5, 5½, 5½, 6)" [11.5 (11.5, 11.5, 12.5, 12.5, 14, 14, 15) cm] from underarm, ending after a WS row.

Join side panels to center

Next row: (RS) Work to last st, pm, p1, return sts held for side panel to LH needle and work in patt to end.
Next row: Work side panel to 1 st before m, k1, work as est to last st, pm, p1, return sts held for side panel to LH needle and work in patt to end—110 (116, 122, 128, 134, 140, 146, 152) sts on needle.

Begin side-body decreases

Next row *double dec row*: (RS) Work as est to m, sl m, k2tog two times, knit to next m, sl m, work to next m, sl m, knit to 4 sts before next m, ssk two times, sl m, work as est to end (4 sts dec'd)—106 (112, 118, 124, 130, 136, 142, 148) sts rem.
Rep *double dec row* every RS row 2 more times—98 (104, 110, 116, 122, 128, 134, 140) sts rem.
Work 1 WS row.
Next row *dec row*: Work to m, sl m, k2tog, knit to next m, sl m, work to next m, sl m, knit to 2 sts before next m, ssk, sl m, work to end (2 sts dec'd)—96 (102, 108, 114, 120, 126, 132, 138) sts rem.
Rep *dec row* every RS row 17 more times—62 (68, 74, 80, 86, 92, 98, 104) sts rem.
Next row: (WS) Bind off knitwise as follows: BO 5, drop next purl st, (yo, pass last BO st over yo to BO) four times, BO 7 sts, drop next purl st, (yo, pass last BO st over yo to BO) four times, BO to last m, BO 7, drop next purl st, (yo, pass last BO st over yo to BO) four times, BO 7 sts, drop next purl st (yo, pass last BO st over yo to BO) four times, BO to end.
Unravel each dropped purl st until it reaches the CO edge.

FINISHING

Weave in ends. Wet block tank to finished measurements.
Sew side seams using the mattress stitch.
Sew BO and CO edges together at each underarm.

Increases along bottom edge of front body 'push' godet stitches outward; decreases along bottom edge of back 'pull' godet stitches in toward center.

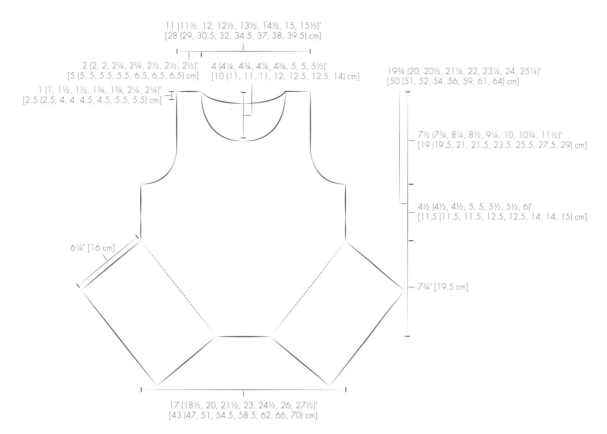

11 (11½, 12, 12½, 13½, 14½, 15, 15½)"
[28 (29, 30.5, 32, 34.5, 37, 38, 39.5) cm]

2 (2, 2, 2¼, 2¼, 2½, 2½, 2½)"
[5 (5, 5, 5.5, 5.5, 6.5, 6.5, 6.5) cm]

4 (4¼, 4¼, 4¼, 4¾, 5, 5, 5½)"
[10 (11, 11, 11, 12, 12.5, 12.5, 14) cm]

19¾ (20, 20½, 21¼, 22, 23¼, 24, 25¼)"
[50 (51, 52, 54, 56, 59, 61, 64) cm]

1 (1, 1½, 1½, 1¾, 1¾, 2¼, 2¼)"
[2.5 (2.5, 4, 4, 4.5, 4.5, 5.5, 5.5) cm]

7½ (7¾, 8¼, 8½, 9¼, 10, 10¾, 11½)"
[19 (19.5, 21, 21.5, 23.5, 25.5, 27.5, 29) cm]

4½ (4½, 4½, 5, 5, 5½, 5½, 6)"
[11.5 (11.5, 11.5, 12.5, 12.5, 14, 14, 15) cm]

6¼" [16 cm]

7¾" [19.5 cm]

17 (18½, 20, 21½, 23, 24½, 26, 27½)"
[43 (47, 51, 54.5, 58.5, 62, 66, 70) cm]

Gambrel

Sleeves play a starring role in this unusual, summery pullover. Picked up around each armhole, Gambrel's sleeves alternate lace ladder rings in Sparrow with simple dropped stitches in Kestrel, the main yarn. As they circle the upper arm, they make concentric circles. For a smooth shoulder, the front pieces extend a few inches past the top of the shoulder onto the back where they're angled with short rows to lie smooth and flat against the shoulder blades.

FINISHED MEASUREMENTS

30½ (32½, 35½, 38½, 41½, 44½, 47½, 50½)"
[77.5 (82.5, 90.25, 97.75, 105.5, 113, 120.75, 128.25) cm] bust circumference; shown in size 32½" [82.5 cm] with 1½" [4 cm] negative ease

YARN

Kestrel by Quince & Co
(100% organic linen; 76yd [70m]/50g)
5 (6, 6, 7, 8, 9, 10, 11) skeins
Anemone 513 (MC)
and
Sparrow by Quince & Co
(100% organic linen; 168yd [155m]/50g)
1 (1, 2, 2, 2, 2, 2, 2) skeins Paprika 210 (CC)

NEEDLES

One 32" circular needle (circ) in size US 9 [5.5 mm]
One spare circ in size US 9 [5.5 mm]
One 24" circ in size US 6 [4 mm]
One 24" circ in size US 4 [3.5 mm]
Or size to obtain gauge

NOTIONS

Stitch markers
Waste yarn
Tapestry needle
Crochet hook in size US 1 [5.5 mm]

GAUGE

16 sts and 24 rows = 4" [10 cm] in stockinette stitch with largest needles, after wet blocking.

CONSTRUCTION NOTES

Pullover is worked flat, center front to center front, to underarm, then separated for fronts and back. Sleeve stitches are picked up around armhole and worked in alternating patterns with Sparrow and Kestrel, ending with a rib trim. Sleeves are seamed and a single crochet edging is worked along fronts and back neck, then fronts are joined using chain and slip stitches.

SPECIAL ABBREVIATIONS

yo2 (yarn over twice / double yarnover): Bring yarn over needle twice.
sl 1: Slip 1 stitch purlwise with yarn to the WS of work.
m1-p/R (make 1 purlwise right slanting): Insert LH needle from back to front under horizontal strand between stitch just worked and next stitch, purl lifted strand through the front loop (1 stitch increased).
m1-p/L (make 1 purlwise left slanting): Insert LH needle from front to back under horizontal strand between stitch just worked and next stitch, purl lifted strand through the back loop (1 stitch increased).
spp: Slip 1 stitch knitwise to RH needle, p1, pass slipped stitch over (1 stitch decreased).
skp: Slip 1 stitch knitwise to RH needle, k1, pass slipped stitch over (1 stitch decreased).
ch (chain): Wrap the yarn around the crochet hook (yarn over) and draw it through the loop on the hook to form the first chain. Rep this step as many times as instructed. (The loop on the hook is never included when counting the number of chains.)
sl st (slip stitch): Insert crochet hook in the indicated stitch, yarn over and draw through both the stitch and the loop on the hook.
sc (single crochet): Insert crochet hook in indicated stitch, yarn over and pull up a loop, yarn over and draw through both loops on hook.

TECHNIQUES

yo short rows (see page 29 for detailed instructions)
(WS) With yarn behind RH needle, purl the first stitch, bringing the yarn over the top of RH needle, creating an extra stitch.
(RS) With yarn in front of RH needle, knit the first stitch, bringing the yarn over the top of RH needle, creating an extra stitch.

PULLOVER

Begin at bottom edge

With MC and largest circular needle (circ), and using the long-tail cast on, CO 137 (145, 157, 169, 181, 193, 205, 217) sts. Do not join.

First row *place markers*: (WS) Beg at center front, p34 (36, 39, 42, 45, 48, 51, 54), place marker (pm) for side, p69 (73, 79, 85, 91, 97, 103, 109), pm for side, p34 (36, 39, 42, 45, 48, 51, 54) sts to end.

Begin stockinette

Next row: (RS) Knit.

Cont in St st until pc meas 3" [7.5 cm] from beg, ending after a WS row.

Begin side shaping

Next row *dec row*: (RS) *Knit to 4 sts before marker (m), ssk, k2, slip marker (sl m), k2, k2tog; rep from * one more time, knit to end (4 sts dec'd)—133 (141, 153, 165, 177, 189, 201, 213) sts rem.

Rep *dec row* every 10 (10, 10, 12, 12, 12, 14, 14) rows 3 more times—121 (129, 141, 153, 165, 177, 189, 201) sts rem.

Work even until pc meas 10 (10, 10, 11, 11, 11, 12, 12)" [25.5 (25.5, 25.5, 28, 28, 28, 30.5, 30.5) cm] from beg, ending after a WS row.

Separate fronts and back

Next row: (RS) Knit across right front to m, then place sts for back onto waste yarn and rem sts for left front onto separate waste yarn—30 (32, 35, 38, 41, 44, 47, 50) sts rem for right front.

Begin right front armhole shaping

Next row: (WS) BO 4 sts, purl to end—26 (28, 31, 34, 37, 40, 43, 46) sts rem.

Next row: Knit.

Next row: Spp, BO 3 sts, purl to end—22 (24, 27, 30, 33, 36, 39, 42) sts rem.

Work 1 RS row.

Next row: Spp, BO 2 sts, purl to end—19 (21, 24, 27, 30, 33, 36, 39) sts rem.

Work 1 RS row.

Next row: Spp, BO 1 st, purl to end—17 (19, 22, 25, 28, 31, 34, 37) sts rem.

Rep the last 2 rows 2 more times—13 (15, 18, 21, 24, 27, 30, 33) sts rem.

Next row *dec row*: (RS) Knit to last 3 sts, ssk, k1 (1 st dec'd)—12 (14, 17, 20, 23, 26, 29, 32) sts rem.

Rep *dec row* every RS row 3 more times, every 4 rows 2 times, then every 6 rows 1 time—6 (8, 11, 14, 17, 20, 23, 26) sts rem.

Work even until right front meas 10½ (10½, 11½, 11½, 12½, 12½, 13½, 13½)" [26.5 (26.5, 29, 29, 32, 32, 34.5, 34.3) cm] from underarm, ending after a WS row at top of shoulder.

Begin back neck shaping

Next row *inc row*: (RS) K1, M1L, knit to end (1 st inc'd)—7 (9, 12, 15, 18, 21, 24, 27) sts.

Rep *inc row* every 4 rows 2 more times—9 (11, 14, 17, 20, 23, 26, 29) sts.

Work 1 WS row.

Begin short row shaping for extended shoulder piece

Next row *short row 1*: (RS) K1, M1L, knit to last 2 (3, 3, 5, 5, 5, 6, 6) sts, turn; (WS) yo, purl to end (1 st inc'd).

Next row *short row 2*: (RS) K1, M1L, knit to 3 (3, 4, 4, 5, 6, 6, 7) sts before last yo, turn; (WS) yo, purl to end (1 st inc'd).

Rep *short row 2* two more times—13 (15, 18, 21, 24, 27, 30, 33) sts.

Next row: (RS) Knit to end, and as you reach each yarnover, k2tog with next stitch. Cut yarn. Place sts onto waste yarn.

Back

Return 61 (65, 71, 77, 83, 89, 95, 101) sts held for back to larger circ. Join yarn ready to work a RS row.

Begin armhole shaping (decreases)

Next row: (RS) BO 4 sts, knit to end.

Next row: BO 4 sts, purl to end—53 (57, 63, 69, 75, 81, 87, 93) sts rem.

Next row: (RS) Skp, BO 3 sts, knit to end.

Next row: Spp, BO 3 sts, purl to end—45 (49, 55, 61, 67, 73, 79, 85) sts rem.

Next row: (RS) Skp, BO 2 sts, knit to end.

Next row: Spp, BO 2 sts, purl to end—39 (43, 49, 55, 61, 67, 73, 79) sts rem.

Next row: (RS) Skp, BO 1 st, knit to end.

Next row: Spp, BO 1 st, purl to end—35 (39, 45, 51, 57, 63, 69, 75) sts rem.

Rep the last 2 rows 1 more time—31 (35, 41, 47, 53, 59, 65, 71) sts rem.

Next row *dec row*: (RS) K1, k2tog, knit to last 3 sts, ssk, k1 (2 sts dec'd)—29 (33, 39, 45, 51, 57, 63, 69) sts rem.

Rep *dec row* every RS row 3 more times, every 4 rows 2 times, then every 6 rows 1 time—17 (21, 27, 33, 39, 45, 51, 57) sts rem.

Work 5 (5, 11, 11, 17, 17, 23, 23) rows even.

Continue armhole shaping (increases)

Next row *inc row*: (RS) K1, M1L, knit to last st, M1R, k1 (2 sts inc'd)—19 (23, 29, 35, 41, 47, 53, 59) sts.

Rep *inc row* every 6 rows 1 more time, every 4 rows 2 times, then every RS row 3 times—31 (35, 41, 47, 53, 59, 65, 71) sts.

Cut yarn. Place sts onto waste yarn.

LEFT FRONT

Return sts held for left front to largest circ. Join yarn ready to work a RS row.

Begin armhole shaping

Next row: (RS) BO 4 sts, knit to end—26 (28, 31, 34, 37, 40, 43, 46) sts rem.
Next row: Purl.
Next row: Skp, BO 3 sts, knit to end—22 (24, 27, 30, 33, 36, 39, 42) sts rem.
Work 1 WS row.
Next row: Skp, BO 2 sts, knit to end—19 (21, 24, 27, 30, 33, 36, 39) sts rem.
Work 1 WS row.
Next row: Skp, BO 1 st, knit to end—17 (19, 22, 25, 28, 31, 34, 37) sts rem.
Work 1 WS row.
Rep the last 2 rows 2 more times—13 (15, 18, 21, 24, 27, 30, 33) sts rem.
Next row *dec row*: (RS) Knit to last 3 sts, ssk, k1 (1 st dec'd)—12 (14, 17, 20, 23, 26, 29, 32) sts rem.
Rep *dec row* every RS row 3 more times, every 4 rows 2 times, then every 6 rows 1 time—6 (8, 11, 14, 17, 20, 23, 26) sts rem.
Work even until left front meas 10½ (10½, 11½, 11½, 12½, 12½, 13½, 13½)" [26.5 (26.5, 29, 29, 32, 32, 34.5, 34.3) cm] from underarm, ending after a WS row.

Begin back neck shaping

Next row *inc row*: (RS) Knit to last st, M1R, k1 (1 st inc'd)—7 (9, 12, 15, 18, 21, 24, 27) sts.
Rep *inc row* every 4 rows 2 more times—9 (11, 14, 17, 20, 23, 26, 29) sts.
Work 2 rows even.

Begin short row shaping for extended shoulder piece

Next row *short row 1*: (WS) Purl to last 2 (3, 3, 5, 5, 5, 6, 6) sts, turn; (RS) yo, knit to last st, M1R, k1 (1 st inc'd).
Next row *short row 2*: (WS) Purl to 3 (3, 4, 4, 5, 6, 6, 7) sts before last yo, turn; (RS) yo, knit to last st, M1R, k1 (1 st inc'd).
Rep *short row 2* two more times—13 (15, 18, 21, 24, 27, 30, 33) sts.
Next row: (WS) Purl to end, and as you reach each yarnover, ssp with the next stitch.

FINISHING

Weave in ends. Wet block pullover to finished measurements.

Join shoulders

Place sts for back onto spare largest circ. With RS of pcs tog and using the three-needle bind off, BO all left front sts with their back sts, BO back sts until 13 (15, 18, 21, 24, 27, 30, 33) sts rem on LH needle, return sts for right front to circ and with RS of pcs tog and using the three-needle bind off, BO rem sts.

Exaggerated armhole shaping creates plenty of room for dramatic sleeves.

Sleeves

With MC and smallest circ, beg at center of underarm, pick up and knit 108 (108, 118, 118, 128, 128, 138, 138) sts along armhole edge (1 st in each BO st and approx 4 sts for every 5 rows). Do not join.

Change to CC, but do not cut MC.

Begin lace ladder

Using the cable cast on, CO 6 sts.

Next row: (RS) K1, k2tog, yo2, ssk, p2tog (last ladder st with next picked-up st), turn.

Next row: P2, (p1, k1) in yo2, p2.

Rep the last 2 rows until all picked up sts have been used, ending after a RS row.

Next row: (WS) Bind off purlwise (working p1, k1 into yo2).

Begin drop stitch pattern

With attached MC (loosely to not pucker CC ladder) and largest circ, pick up and knit 109 (109, 119, 119, 129, 129, 139, 139) sts along side edge of CC ladder (approx 1 st for every 2 rows). Do not join.

Next row: (WS) *P1, yo2; rep from * to last st, p1.

Next row: Knit to end, carefully dropping each yo as you go—109 (109, 119, 119, 129, 129, 139, 139) sts.

Next row: Knit.

Change to smallest circ and join CC ready to work another WS row, but do not cut MC.

Next row: (WS) With CC, *p2, p2tog; rep from * to last 1 (1, 3, 3, 1, 1, 3, 3) st(s), purl to end—82 (82, 90, 90, 97, 97, 105, 105) sts rem.

Repeat lace ladder

Begin drop stitch pattern

With attached MC and largest circ, pick up and knit 83 (83, 91, 91, 98, 98, 106, 106) sts along side edge of CC ladder. Do not join.

Next row: (WS) *P1, yo2; rep from * to last st, p1.

Next row: Knit to end, carefully dropping each yo as you go—83 (83, 91, 91, 98, 98, 106, 106) sts.

Next row: Knit.

Change to smallest circ and join CC ready to work another WS row, but do not cut MC.

Next row: (WS) With CC, *p2, p2tog; rep from * to last 3 (3, 3, 3, 2, 2, 2, 2) sts, purl to end—63 (63, 69, 69, 74, 74, 80, 80) sts rem.

Alternating rows of lace ladders in Sparrow and dropped stitches in Kestrel form concentric circles when seamed at the underarm.

Repeat lace ladder

Begin drop stitch pattern
With attached MC and largest circ, pick up and knit 64 (64, 70, 70, 75, 75, 81, 81) along side edge of CC ladder. Do not join.
Next row: (WS) *P1, yo2; rep from * to last st, p1.
Next row: Knit to end, carefully dropping each yo as you go—64 (64, 70, 70, 75, 75, 81, 81) sts.
Next row: Knit.
Change to smallest circ and join CC ready to work another WS row, but do not cut MC.
Next row: (WS) With CC, *p2, p2tog; rep from * to last 4 (4, 2, 2, 3, 3, 1, 1) st(s), purl to end—49 (49, 53, 53, 57, 57, 61, 61) sts rem.

Repeat lace ladder

Begin ribbed cuff
With attached MC and middle-sized circ, pick up and knit 50 (50, 54, 54, 58, 58, 62, 62) sts along side edge of CC ladder. Do not join.
Next row: (WS) *P2, k2; rep from * to last 2 sts, p2.
Next row: *K2, p2; rep from * to last 2 sts, k2.
Cont in est rib for 1½" [4 cm].
Next row: Bind off in pattern.

Crochet neck trim
With MC and hook, beg at lower right front neck edge, sc along right front to shoulder seam (1 st for every 2 rows), sc along back neck (1 st in each BO st), then sc along left front to end.
Next row: (RS) Join fronts as follows: Ch 1, sl st in first sc on right front, *ch 1, sk 1 sc, sl st in next sc on left front, ch 1, sk 1 sc, sl st in next sc on right front; rep from * until 13" [33 cm] of fronts are joined. Fasten off.

Sew sleeve seams. Weave in remaining ends. Block again, if you like.

Extended front pieces make a smooth line at top of shoulders.

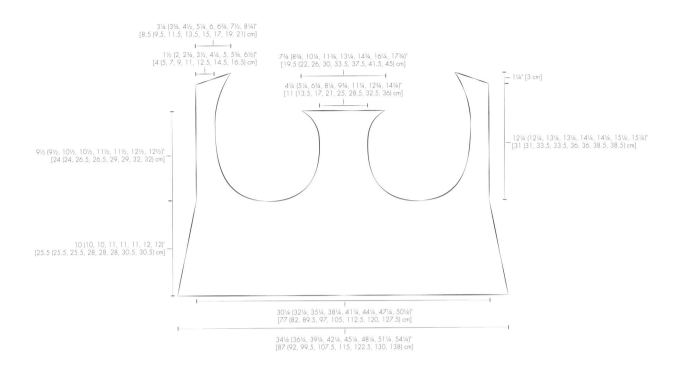

3¼ (3¾, 4½, 5¼, 6, 6¾, 7½, 8¼)"
[8.5 (9.5, 11.5, 13.5, 15, 17, 19, 21) cm]

1½ (2, 2¾, 3½, 4¼, 5, 5¾, 6½)"
[4 (5, 7, 9, 11, 12.5, 14.5, 16.5) cm]

7¾ (8¾, 10¼, 11¾, 13¼, 14¾, 16¼, 17¾)"
[19.5 (22, 26, 30, 33.5, 37.5, 41.5, 45) cm]

4¼ (5¼, 6¾, 8¼, 9¾, 11¼, 12¾, 14¼)"
[11 (13.5, 17, 21, 25, 28.5, 32.5, 36) cm]

1¼" [3 cm]

9½ (9½, 10½, 10½, 11½, 11½, 12½, 12½)"
[24 (24, 26.5, 26.5, 29, 29, 32, 32) cm]

12¼ (12¼, 13¼, 13¼, 14¼, 14¼, 15¼, 15¼)"
[31 (31, 33.5, 33.5, 36, 36, 38.5, 38.5) cm]

10 (10, 10, 11, 11, 11, 12, 12)"
[25.5 (25.5, 25.5, 28, 28, 28, 30.5, 30.5) cm]

30¼ (32¼, 35¼, 38¼, 41¼, 44¼, 47¼, 50¼)"
[77 (82, 89.5, 97, 105, 112.5, 120, 127.5) cm]

34¼ (36¼, 39¼, 42¼, 45¼, 48¼, 51¼, 54¼)"
[87 (92, 99.5, 107.5, 115, 122.5, 130, 138) cm]

THE MIGHTY RECTANGLE

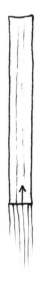

① Perimeter is the most basic of rectangles, in this case, a long and narrow one. Knit it narrow end to narrow end, but don't ignore the possibilities in knitting wide to wide.

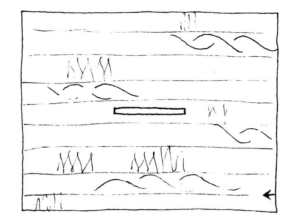

② Dormer is a rectangle turned on its side and worked from cuff edge to cuff edge. A simple slit in the center makes a neck opening. Knitted side-to-side, the cable panel runs horizontally on this piece.

In Gambrel, circles meet the rectangle. The front and back pieces can be imagined as bodice-sized rectangles. But at the armhole, instead of the standard cutaway that lines up the side of the piece with the width of the shoulder, Norah has carved out large circles. For sleeves, she picked up stitches around the armhole edge and worked rows of alternating patterns, which appear as concentric circles when the sleeve is seamed.

sleeve "top" view

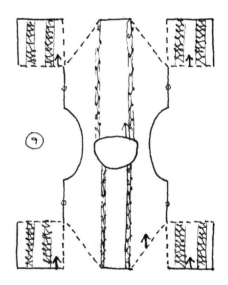

⑨

⑩

side view

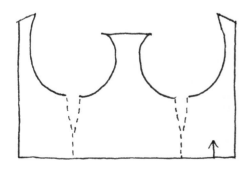

Annex makes use of rectangles in an unexpected way. Although they look rounded and drapey, Annex's hip godets are simple, untinkered rectangles, positioned in such a way that they fall gracefully over the hip. The sweater's body is itself a long rectangle that folds at the shoulder; curves are carved out for the fitted armholes and neck.

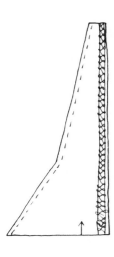

③

Spate is a rectangle turned triangle by way of decreases. Spate's shaped edge isn't a straight line, however. Instead, the angle changes by way of decreases every other row to every 4th row to every 6th row.

Cella couldn't be simpler. One large rectangle folded origami-style to make openings for the arm.

④

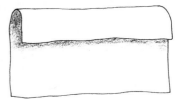

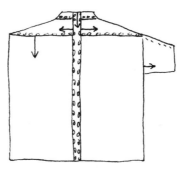

front   back

⑤

Arena is a pieced-together rectangle. Rather than working from the bottom up, the yoke is worked in pieces knitted in different directions. Then the main section of the back (rectangle!) is picked up from the yoke and knitted down. A line of increases along the center fronts turns these pieces from simple rectangles to ones with an angled edge.

⑧

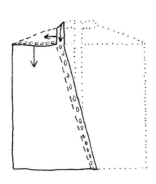

⑦

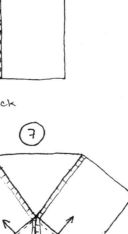

⑥

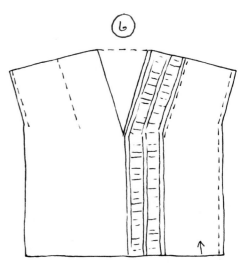

It's easy to see from the illustration that Bower is a single rectangle folded at the shoulder. A long, slender triangle is cut out of the back for a deep V-neck. A few stitches added on the front half and decreased on the back make short, loose sleeves.

Arris begins at the bottom edge as a rectangle, but decreases along the side edges shape it into a flat point. Stitches picked up along the sloped edge and knitted up form smaller rectangles, which, because of their angle relative to the body, create slanted shoulders.

Walkway is made from two separate rectangles joined at the shoulder. Each has a slit for the V-neck. Angling the shoulders (top edge of the rectangle), rather than leaving them straight, allows the sweater to hang without folds under the arm.

Techniques

k2tog: Knit 2 stitches together (1 stitch decreased, leans to the right).

k3tog: Knit 3 stitches together (2 stitches decreased, leans to the right).

ssk (slip, slip, knit): Slip 2 stitches one at a time knitwise to the RH needle; return stitches to LH needle in turned position and knit them together through the back loops (1 stitch decreased, leans to the left).

sssk (slip, slip, slip, knit): Slip 3 stitches one at a time knitwise to the RH needle; return stitches to LH needle in turned position and knit them together through the back loops (2 stitches decreased, leans to the left).

p2tog: Purl 2 stitches together (1 stitch decreased).

ssp (slip, slip, purl): Slip 2 stitches one at a time knitwise to the RH needle; return stitches to LH needle in turned position and purl them together through the back loops (1 stitch decreased).

p1-f/b (purl 1, front and back): Purl into the front loop, then the back loop of next stitch (1 stitch increased).

p3tog: Purl 3 stitches together (2 stitches decreased).

m1 (make 1): Insert LH needle from front to back under horizontal strand between stitch just worked and next stitch, knit lifted strand through the back loop (1 stitch increased).

M1L (make 1 left slanting): Insert LH needle from front to back under horizontal strand between stitch just worked and next stitch, knit lifted strand through the back loop (1 stitch increased).

M1R (make 1 right slanting): Insert LH needle from back to front under horizontal strand between stitch just worked and next stitch, knit lifted strand through the front loop (1 stitch increased).

k1-tbl: Knit 1 stitch through the back loop to twist stitch.

p1-tbl: Purl 1 stitch through the back loop to twist stitch.

yo (yarnover): Bring yarn over needle and work the next stitch. See page 15 for specifics.

yo2 (yarn over twice or double yarnover): Bring yarn over needle twice.

Duplicate stitch for weaving in ends

The best way to secure your ends when working with linen is to weave them in on the wrong side of the fabric in a way that mimics the stitches.

Thread your yarn end onto a tapestry needle. With the wrong (purl) side of the piece facing up:

1. Begin by bringing your needle up through the upside-down U of the nearest purl stitch. (Stitch looks like a frown.)

2. From here, bring your needle up through the U-shaped stitch above and slightly to the left of the frown stitch you just used. (Stitch looks like a smile.) Then, from the top down, bring needle down through the U-shaped stitch to the left of the one just worked and return through the first frown stitch.

3. From the bottom up, bring your needle up into the frown stitch to the left of the one just worked, then still from the bottom up, return through the same smile stitch worked in the row above.

Repeat Steps 2 and 3 through four or five more stitches. Take care not to work your stitches too tightly. The tension should match that of the knit fabric to avoid puckering.

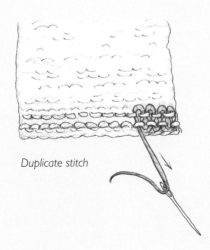

Duplicate stitch

Standard Abbreviations

approx	approximately
beg	begin(ning)
BO	bind off
CO	cast on
circ	circular needle
cm	centimeter(s)
cn	cable needle
cont	continue
dec('d)	decrease(d)
est	established
g	gram(s)
inc('d)	increase(d)
k	knit
LH	left hand
meas	measures
mm	millimeter(s)
m	marker(s)
p	purl
patt(s)	pattern(s)
pc(s)	piece(s)
pm	place marker
rem	remain(ing); remain(s)
rep	repeat(ing); repeat(s)
RH	right hand
RS	right side
sk	skip
sl m	slip marker
St st	stockinette stitch
st(s)	stitch(es)
tbl	through the back loop
tog	together
WS	wrong side
yd	yard(s)

Norah Gaughan

Raised by artists in the wilds of the Hudson Valley (her father was a well known science fiction illustrator in his day), Norah was immersed in both art and the needle arts from an early age and honed her skills participating in 4-H for much of her childhood. One of those annoying students who always sat in the front row and raised her hand too much, Norah went on to earn a degree in Biology and Art from Brown University. During the years that followed she concentrated on her greatest love, knitting. She worked first as a freelancer for yarn companies and knitting magazines, then as the design director at JCA and, more recently, at Berroco, where she headed up the design team and published sixteen eponymous booklets. Norah's upbringing, schooling, and experience coalesce in her two hardcover volumes *Knitting Nature* and *Norah Gaughan's Knitted Cable Sourcebook*.

Having studied both art and science, Norah loves it when the two intersect, as they do in this volume, *Framework*, where geometry is an integral part of the designs.

Acknowledgements

Many thanks to the following people for their help in putting this book together:

Dawn Catanzaro and Jerusha Robinson for sizing and tech editing the patterns and for understanding how my brain works,
Pam Allen for photography, layout, and general help,
Leila Raabe for technical illustrations,
Whitney Hayward for botanical illustrations,
Manaan Alexander, Meghan Lynch, and Taylor Sikes (from Port City Models) for modeling,
and, of course, Elke Probst, Patricia McMullen, Marie Harriman, Nancy Brown, and Martha Wissing, my knitters.